The Si[lent State]

Heather Brooke is a freelance journalist and Freedom of Information campaigner based in London who is famous for uncovering the MPs' expenses scandal. She writes for all the main national papers and has worked as a consultant and presenter for Channel 4's *Dispatches*. She is a visiting professor at City University's Department of Journalism and is also the author of *Your Right to Know*. In 2009 she was named Reformer of the Year and has won numerous awards for her work, including the Setting the Political Agenda Award from the Political Studies Association and, in March 2010, the Judges' Prize at the British Press Awards.

Praise for *The Silent State*

'Anyone with a vote worth stealing should read this. You won't know whether to laugh or rise up and overthrow absolutely everything.'

Charlie Brooker

'A wonderful book . . . Heather Brooke puts every other British journalist to shame. She has changed British public culture and earned an essential place in our national history. She is an extraordinary figure who must be celebrated.'

Peter Oborne, *Daily Mail*

'Secrecy is one of the great British diseases. It's so secret that we don't even admit we suffer from it. Heather Brooke is part of the cure – challenging the routine concealment and distortion of important information. There should be more journalists doing the same.'

3|2210570 .

…t *Earth News*

'Passionate, eloquent and persuasive . . . We need the likes of Heather Brooke to challenge, to take up grievances and to campaign.'

Peter Riddell, *Times Book of the Week*

'Brooke tells the story of . . . one of the most successful raids ever carried out against the Establishment vividly.'

Telegraph

'Entertaining, if shocking.'

Rod Liddle

'Brilliantly explains how and why this extraordinary situation works to the public's disadvantage and what can be done to challenge and change it.'

Ian Hislop

'Brooke, author of *The Silent State*, did more to rid us of a corrupt, anachronistic and unjust system of governance than anyone and, if there is a hero of our troubled political times, it is her.'

Sunday Times

'She's a total ninja.'

Ben Goldacre, author of *Bad Science*

The Silent State

HEATHER BROOKE

 WINDMILL BOOKS

Published by Windmill Books 2011

2 4 6 8 10 9 7 5 3

Copyright © Heather Brooke 2010
Preface to the paperback edition © Heather Brooke 2011

Heather Brooke has asserted her right under the Copyright, Designs and
Patents Act 1988, to be identified as the author of this work.

This book is sold subject to the condition that it shall not, by way of
trade or otherwise, be lent, resold, hired out, or otherwise circulated without
the publisher's prior consent in any form of binding or cover other than that
in which it is published and without a similar condition including this
condition being imposed on the subsequent purchaser.

First published in Great Britain in 2010 by William Heinemann

Windmill Books
The Random House Group Limited
20 Vauxhall Bridge Road, London SW1V 2SA

Addresses for companies within The Random House Group Limited can
be found at: www.randomhouse.co.uk/offices.htm

The Random House Group Limited Reg. No. 954009

www.rbooks.co.uk

A CIP catalogue record for this book
is available from the British Library

ISBN 9780099537625

The Random House Group Limited supports The Forest Stewardship
Council (FSC), the leading international forest certification organisation.
All our titles that are printed on Greenpeace approved FSC certified paper
carry the FSC logo. Our paper procurement policy can be found at
www.rbooks.co.uk/environment

Mixed Sources
Product group from well-managed
forests and other controlled sources
www.fsc.org Cert no. TT-COC-2139
© 1996 Forest Stewardship Council

Typeset in Minion by Palimpsest Book Production Limited,
Falkirk, Stirlingshire
Printed and bound in Great Britain by CPI Cox & Wyman, Reading RG1 8EX

To whistleblowers

past, present, future

Contents

CONTENTS

Preface to the paperback edition

It's not every day an author gets to hear her ideas coming from the mouth of an incoming Deputy Prime Minister. But that is exactly the experience I had on 19 May 2010 as I listened to Nick Clegg's speech on the Big Society, in which he promised that 'this government is going to trust the people', criticised the 'intrusive' nature of the state and pledged to govern in an 'open, transparent [and] decent' manner. I don't know if *The Silent State* was bedtime reading for politicians in the run up to the general election, but the concluding chapter of this book – Manifesto for a New Democracy – now reads like a blueprint for the future.

However, what politicians say and what they do are two completely different things, and we'd be wise to focus on what actually gets done rather than what people in power say they will do. With that in mind, here are some things that have changed in Britain since *The Silent State* was first published in April 2010.

The alarmingly intrusive children's database Contactpoint, which I discuss in Chapter 1, was abolished on 6 August 2010 and we may all breathe a little easier for that. However, each local authority has its own mini Contactpoint and no one has mentioned abolishing these. Given the poor standard of data handling in local councils, it's now time to ask these councils about the data they hold on children. The centralised Common Assessment Framework (e-CAF) database that holds the profiles of children needing services (that's about 4 million kids, or ⅓ of the child population) remains also. These aren't just children on welfare but those with disabilities, who need learning support, or who receive any sort of state health or education entitlement. As the children's rights campaigner Terri Dowty, whom we'll meet in Chapter 1, says: 'The shop window is gone but the shop is still there.'

The National Identity Register and ID card scheme have been scrapped, the police can no longer keep the DNA of innocent people and the government has suspended the vetting database I mention in Chapter 7. All of these are major victories for individual privacy. However, a new problem has emerged with increasing demands by the police and others for us to 'show our papers' before entering certain venues or buying certain goods. Furthermore, the Independent Safeguarding Authority is up and running and currently making decisions about who should be barred from working with children. A review is ongoing to determine the extent to which the state should regulate trust relation-ships between private people. Meanwhile, privatisation of public information through the lucrative trade in criminal records continues, with the Criminal Records Bureau alone processing 4.5 million checks a year.

The London Datastore and Data.gov.uk have taken up the call to give back the people's data to the people (see Chapter 5) and have successfully brought a large amount of Ordnance Survey maps, along with many other datasets, into the public domain. As I argue in the following pages, such opening up of official data leads to innovation and already a number of websites have emerged to help the public make sense of this new data, such as Where Does My Money Go?, OpenlyLocal and Armchair Auditor.

Another big change relates to how public money is spent. Money tells you where power lies and we can't make any kind of informed decision without access to detailed line-item budgets that tell us exactly where our taxes are going. There have been some terrific advances here. In June 2010 the historic COINS database was opened to the public. This details how the Treasury is distributing money to various departments and public bodies. Its value will increase as more live data is put online. The goal is for the public to be able to track where their money goes from the Treasury right down to the smallest council, police force, hospital or school.

Other things we can expect to see from central government include the publication of new government tender documents and contracts; breakdowns of all spending above £25,000; crime data published at a level that allows the public to see what is happening on their streets, and the names, grades, job titles and annual pay rates for most senior civil servants with salaries above £150,000. (This is a start but in Chapter 4 I maintain that *all* public servants should be similarly transparent unless there is clear evidence actual harm would result. After all, they work for us.)

What is most encouraging is the mandate on local governments to publish all spending, contracts and tender documents above £500. That should show, among other things, just how much we're subsidising official propaganda (see Chapter 2's exposé of Britain's taxpayer-subsidised PR industry, which I regret to say is still thriving).

Possibly the only chapter in this book not to have inspired

reform is Chapter 6, on the courts. This is a shame as the courts desperately need to modernise. I guess I know where to look for my next big campaign.

Despite much progress, then, there remain severe problems at the heart of our democracy. Official spokespeople for public institutions are still demanding and being granted anonymity by the press for no good reason (and many bad ones). A number of the databases uncovered in Chapter 1 still exist, and many politicians still dispute the importance of Freedom of Information, meaning the imbalance remains between government transparency and scrutiny of the private individual. Slough Borough Council showed neither shame nor sense by appealing Jane Clift's victory against the silent state (see Chapter 7) – a verdict was still outstanding when this edition went to press. And in relation to the final chapter about my battle with parliament over MPs' expenses, the saga continues, with MPs trying to avoid criminal charges through parliamentary privilege. As you will see, I was never a fan of the Independent Parliamentary Standards Authority. It was a half-baked proposal presented by Harriet Harman. I would much rather have seen the recommendations by Sir Christopher Kelly's public inquiry taken up. The solution to this particular problem remains the same: direct transparency of those claiming public money to the public supplying it.

Yet it's not all doom and gloom. Change happens if we desire it and go after it with enough tenacity. For those dispirited into apathy remember that by doing nothing you are, in fact, doing something. You are supporting the status quo. By doing something, no matter how small, you shift the odds in your favour.

Foreword

A Warning to the Purchaser

You have paid for this book but I am afraid you are not allowed to read the contents. A few other people are allowed to read the contents and under certain circumstances they may choose to tell you about what is in the book. Or not. Even if they do, you have no way of knowing whether what they tell you is accurate. It may be or it may not be. You might in certain circumstances apply to these other people for permission to read the book yourself, but unfortunately you are likely to be refused. You are not entitled to know the grounds on which the other people have decided that you are not allowed to read the book. Sadly, the fact that you have paid for the book is in no way relevant to your right to read it. However, by paying for the book you have agreed that the publishers are entitled to know every detail of your personal life and to use this information in any way that they see fit. Again, I am afraid you are not allowed to know anything about any of the details of any of this at all. The best thing for you to do is to put the book down and think no further about it. Do not attempt to read it illegally as this may result in prosecution and/or imprisonment.

* * *

If this was the deal with a book publisher you would be furious. Yet Heather Brooke demonstrates that this is essentially the deal you make with the entire British government and all the information held by the apparatus of the state. She brilliantly explains how and why this extraordinary situation works to the public's disadvantage and what can be done to challenge it and change it.

Another Warning to the Purchaser

You *are* of course allowed to read this book. And I think you should. But I do have to warn you that as a British taxpayer, you may end up, if not furious, then certainly pretty cross.

Ian Hislop

Introduction

*The most hateful of all names in an English ear is
Nosey Parker.*
George Orwell, *The Lion and the Unicorn*

The government wants to know everything about us but
what do we know about it? In an age of spin and state
surveillance what power does the individual have to get to
the truth? How can a seemingly powerless person find out
what's really going on behind the glossy brochures and the
empty rhetoric pumped out by the powerful? No one
believed I had a hope in hell with my campaign to open up
Parliament but I carried on regardless. I'm stubborn like
that. I'm also pretty nosey.

I write this book as a self-confessed nosey parker. In my
defence, I'd say that my nosiness is focused not on the private
lives of my fellow citizens (though I'm not above twitching
the occasional curtain) but rather on what goes on behind
the big grey buttresses of British bureaucracy. A fine thing
to construct a career out of, you may think. But look at it
this way: do you find things unjust or unfair? Have you ever
thought: 'Someone ought to do something'? Or maybe you're

simply curious to know why something happened the way it did.

What I've learned is that there is no magic person or institution that waves a wand and makes us better or safer. Rather, it is you and me – each of us as individual citizens. Society is only as good as those willing to stand up and ask questions of the people in power and hold them individually accountable for the decisions they make in our name and with our money. Although I scored a coup in my five-year battle to force MPs to disclose their expenses, there is much more that could be achieved if more people asked more questions and demanded better democracy. Britain may be 'the mother of all parliaments' but in reality this country trades on a mythical view of itself, because basic information paid for by the public and collected in our name is off-limits to the very people it is meant to benefit.

Did you know that until October 2007 it was illegal for a fireman to tell the public the results of a fire safety inspection of a local theatre or school? Is it not outrageous that a nurse who blew the whistle on substandard practices in a hospital was struck off? Why do council food safety departments refuse to release details of the restaurants which garner the most food-poisoning complaints? This is information collected on behalf of the public and yet we are routinely the last to know. We have a government (central and local) and criminal justice system that eats up public money and yet the majority of decision-makers remain anonymous and thus free from taking any individual responsibility.

The Internet has allowed us to compare and collect information all across the world. We are able to compare prices between shops and even countries; we get our news globally from thousands of citizen journalists. Yet when it comes to our own government and public services we are forced to accept dumbed-down, pre-packaged propaganda. In spite of what we finally know about MPs' expenses, there remains a great vault of information locked inside public services. Information that *we* paid for.

Increasingly, a class system based on wealth and privilege is being replaced by one based on information. If you are rich enough, powerful enough or politically connected – part of the new information elite – you can access knowledge; if you're none of these things then you'll remain ignorant of how public officials spend public money and make decisions that directly affect your life. If you're the head of a big conglomerate you'll know the names of all the decision-makers in Parliament and likely host lunch for them. If you're Joe Bloggs with a child at a secondary school, you won't even be able to access the staff directory of your local education authority.

Civil servants and those working on behalf of the public have a penchant for protecting their own 'privacy'. By no means, however, will the state be ignorant about you. It will know everything about you and demand not only your money but increasingly all that defines you as an individual. Simultaneous to the government building a database of all our names and biometric information, it is fighting through the courts to stop the public knowing the names and salaries of public officials paid for with public money.

The double standard that now exists between state and private citizen is vastly damaging to democracy. There are laws stopping us taking photographs of the police while they film innocent protestors and compile dossiers for their Forward Intelligence Teams. There are laws preventing us from knowing what goes on in a jury room, or recording the proceedings of a so-called 'open court'. You can't even use a pen in the House of Lords public gallery to record your observations without receiving a stern telling-off by a man in tights. Meanwhile, we are becoming utterly transparent to a battalion of bureaucrats.

This book examines state secrecy and misinformation and what this means for democracy. I will argue that we cannot be an informed electorate without access to information and a right to hold officials to account. And if we're not an informed electorate then we cannot call ourselves a democracy.

What I most want to challenge is the belief that bureaucrats know best. All of history shows they don't. Bureaucracy is a sap on the human spirit. It stifles individual creative drive and, worse, it allows those with power to behave unaccountably and by doing so become corrupted and commit crimes that an individual would find difficult if not impossible.

Few believed me when I said there was something rotten in Parliament. Most people took the view that I was an alarmist, and that things were not so bad. I never said they were awful but what I did say was the system was a guaranteed recipe for profligacy and abuse. There are certain fundamentals of human nature. They don't change and there's nothing rocket sciencey about them. Yet despite their recurring frequency, these simple facts are forgotten:

- Other people's money is remarkably easy to spend.
- The best decisions are those in which the decision-maker is known to those affected by the decisions.

In Chapter 1 I'll look at the rise of surveillance and the millions of pieces of information about you and me that are now held on computers across the land. This is not scare-mongering but an empirical breakdown – the most accurate and comprehensive anywhere – of how our lives are documented by bureaucrats.

Then I'll move on to the rise of corporate public relations as a means to control citizens. Following on from this is the way PR and other insidious tactics such as statistical manipulation are used by the powerful to spin or slant information so that we are unable to judge the effectiveness of a policy or decision.

In Chapter 4 I run rampant through Britain's hallowed corridors of power. I'll explain where the power really lies and how those who have it hide behind noble phrases that really all mean the same thing: power without the responsibility – anonymity. Never a good thing for democracy and I'll explain why.

There's another way of keeping citizens in the dark: make public information too expensive for the people to access. The whole of Europe excels in this and Britain is no exception. In Chapter 5 I'll show you why we're never going to see a British Google. The high cost of civic information reaches its nadir in the justice system, which I take apart in Chapter 6. While we're told justice must be seen to be done, the reality is something quite different. Get ready for a completely behind-the-scenes, unauthorised tour.

From courts to criminals, or rather citizens, but citizens who are now being viewed not as innocent until proved guilty but the reverse. And finally I come to my own epic battle with the state – for MPs' expenses.

I've tried my best to rein in righteousness, which I notice is the danger of these types of books. Instead, I hope the numerous stories I narrate will do more than any righteous rant to illustrate the farcical hypocrisies and absurdities of our current situation. I believe there is a role the state must play to fulfil certain responsibilities vital to the common good such as defence, immigration, justice and education. The only way to ensure these responsibilities are carried out efficiently and for the benefit of the public at large and not for the political elite is through transparency. In the absence of competition, freedom of information is what keeps politicians honest and bureaucrats productive. There is no conflict between wanting transparency for the public official providing a public service and privacy for the private citizen.

All the problems referred to in this book have one single, unifying origin: a fundamental distrust of the common man and woman. A fear not just of 'the masses' but of the regular Joe or Janet. There exists in large sections of British society a belief that human beings are innately bad and only the state can save them. I used to be a crime reporter in the Deep South, so you'd think I'd have as jaded a view of human nature as anyone. But it's the individual I trust, never the state, never an institution, never a bureaucracy. So before we look at the silent state in detail I'd like to examine the bizarre situation we are in now where the state is silent but we – the private citizens – have lost our right to privacy.

1

Somebody's Watching You

The majority of this book is about what we don't know – about the people and institutions that govern us, supposedly in our name, and using our money to do it. The state, however, is by no means ignorant about us, the citizenry. Concurrent with the state's lack of openness is a drive to make *us* totally transparent to officialdom. Civil servants and politicians have built entire careers pushing through projects that peer into private citizens' lives. There are few areas now where we are free from state scrutiny.

In this chapter I'll explore what the state knows about us. After reading, it will be impossible to deny the Information Commissioner's 2006 claim that we are 'sleepwalking into a surveillance society': we'll be accepting it with eyes wide open. To those who repeat the government line 'if you've nothing to fear, you've nothing to hide', I ask this: why won't the government tell us anything? Why won't the Home Office publish its staff directory so we know precisely who does what in a department consistently described by ministers as 'not fit for purpose'? Why is there a pathological aversion to telling the public the exact amount of money spent on big ticket items, the precise reasoning behind decisions of huge national importance, and most crucially the names of all those politicians and officials responsible for the policies that govern us? The reason is simple. Surveillance is not about keeping us safe, it's about power: who has it, and who doesn't. Currently the state has it and citizens don't. Public servants are now our masters.

It's worth pointing out that you will rarely find the details of a surveillance system clearly set out on the face of a bill even though the UK government now spends £16 billion a year on IT projects. Over £100 billion is planned for the next five years in spite of only 30 per cent of these projects succeeding. The Serious Organised Crime Agency inherited more than five hundred databases from other agencies whose functions it took over, and there are thousands of other databases across government. So extensive is the new surveillance bureaucracy that even bureaucrats aren't sure of its extent, and nowhere does there exist a directory of all state surveillance systems, many of which fall foul of privacy and human rights laws.

Some of the most noteworthy Big Britain databases are below but this is far from a definitive list.

- The **National DNA Database** holds the profiles of 4 million people, half a million of whom are innocent. This is the largest DNA database in the world.
- The **NHS detailed care record**, which is the heart of the National Programme for IT, puts our health records online so they are available to the government

and thousands of care providers without, as many clinicians believe, sufficient control or accountability.

- The **Summary Care Record**, also known as the Personal Spine Information Service, holds health data such as allergies and current prescriptions. Controversy arose when it was suggested the police could have access to records. In Scotland, where the Spine is in place, Gordon Brown and Alex Salmond have had their records hacked.
- The **Secondary Care Record** is an archive of clinical data from secondary care.
- The **Police National Computer** holds details of citizens who come to the attention of the police as well as registers of vehicles, criminal offences and property.
- The **Communications Database** holds everyone's itemised phone bills, email headers and mobile phone location histories. Along with the police and HM Revenue & Customs, 510 public authorities can demand access to communications data and 519,260 such requests were made in 2007. From March 2009 ISPs and phone companies were mandated to keep certain communications data for twelve months.
- **Automatic Numberplate Recognition** is accessible by the police, Highways Agency, councils and private firms, scanning 10 million drivers each day.
- There are between 3 million and 4 million **CCTV** cameras in the UK, at least 1.4 million in public spaces. No one knows the precise number because they are not registered. CCTV has taken the largest chunk of the crime prevention budget over the years, eating up 70 per cent of Home Office crime prevention funds which

a Lords report estimated to be in excess of £500 million. No evidence exists to show this surveillance results in more arrests, prosecutions or convictions, and research conducted on prevention shows only limited success in just one or two areas such as vehicle theft. We have the most CCTV of any country on earth and yet the worst amount of antisocial violence in all of Europe.

- The **Driver and Vehicle Licensing Agency** holds data on registered drivers, vehicles and road tax. Although the public are forbidden from accessing these official records, the DVLA does sell them to companies such as wheel clampers even if they have criminal records. In 2007, the *Mail on Sunday* reported the case of the DVLA selling data to two men who were in prison at the time for extorting money from motorists.

- It was data from the **Child Benefits Database** that was lost in November 2007 when two disks were sent through the post containing the records of all UK children and their parents – a total of 25 million people.

- The **Customer Information System** of the Department for Work and Pensions is set to hold 85 million records, harvesting data on everyone who has ever had a National Insurance number. It will include dead people and their beneficiaries. The cost is estimated at £89 million – amazingly one of the cheaper IT projects. Information is available to 80,000 DWP staff, 60,000 users from other government departments and 445 local councils.

- **Identity cards** aren't nearly as intrusive as the underlying database they are linked to: the **National Identity Register** which will hold fifty categories of personal information about each person. For example, the 'address' category isn't just an address where you can be contacted but a list of every address where you have ever lived. Although the government has promised ID cards will be voluntary, all those renewing or applying for passports must be entered on to the National Identity Register. By limiting the methods of payment for registration (you won't be allowed to pay cash), your bank account or credit card details will also be recorded. The way the ID card system was rolled out is typical of all Big Britain databases. The suppliers came in and gave a great presentation about the wonders of biometric technology to technically ignorant politicians and bureaucrats, who bought into an untested idea (it's not *their* money, after all). As Phil Booth, who runs the campaign group No2ID and used to work in the IT sector, argues: 'The whole project is structured in such a way that it's like a piece of internal marketing in which ministers look not at whether the ID card works, or is needed, but how best can they sell it to the public.' Politicians might be losing their enthusiasm for the identity register but bureaucrats haven't. 'The Home Office wants to be gatekeeper to everyone's identity,' Booth says. 'If they control people's identities they would have a phenomenal power base. All other departments would have to go to the Home Office for an individual's official verification. That's the holy grail of bureaucratic power.'

At a time when we know next to nothing about how our government actually operates, officials are engaged in a wholesale attempt to document the entire UK population by collecting our personal data with the ultimate goal, I believe, of taking over our very identity. While this may sound like something out of a dystopian novel, it is by no means an exaggeration. If we keep going at this rate, before long we will all have a 'data doppelgänger' – an official, government-sanctioned version of us. And, as we shall see at the end of this chapter, the onus will be on *us* to justify that we are one and the same as the official version.

When we grant the state such powers we lose a number of democratic rights: to be innocent until proven guilty; to live freely without interference from the authorities; to go about our business without having to justify ourselves to self-important officials. Yet above and beyond such lofty issues as civil liberties and individual rights, the main reason to object to these projects is simply common sense: massive surveillance systems are colossally expensive and simply don't work in the way promised.

Before investigating some of these databases in more detail, it's first worth thinking about how we got here. Why *is* Britain the world capital of state surveillance? Surely that's not the British way. That dubious honour must go to China, North Korea or former East Germany – not Britain, land of cricket, summer fetes and amateurish but relatively harmless politicians (not to mention the Magna Carta, the 1689 Bill of Rights, the Glorious Revolution and the 1832 Reform Act). Aren't we a people who just don't *do* dictatorships?

Although the Second World War did a great deal to shake up the rigid class structure of the past, as Britain stands in the twenty-first century, a true democracy it is not (we still have hereditary peers and bishops in the legislative upper house for goodness' sake). The political elite have never accepted the principle of devolving power right down to individual citizens – it was more than enough to allow the proletariat into the political party system. This compromise allowed for the construction of the welfare state – there might be great social injustices and little social mobility, but at least those at the bottom would not be left to starve or live in squalor without health care. While debate rages about whether or not the welfare state succeeded in destroying the social class system or actually reinforcing it, the resulting shift in attitudes to privacy has often been overlooked.

At the end of the Second World War, one of the first acts by the new United Nations was to draft the Universal Declaration of Human Rights. Article 12 reads:

> No one shall be subjected to arbitrary interference with his privacy, family, home or correspondence, nor to attacks upon his honour and reputation. Everyone has the right to the protection of the law against such interference or attacks.

Straightforward and simple: the state is a menace from which individuals must be protected. It mirrors the absolutism of the First Amendment in the American Bill of Rights:

> Congress shall make no law respecting an establishment of religion, or prohibiting the free exercise thereof; or abridging the freedom of speech, or of the press; or the right of the people peaceably to assemble, and to petition the Government for a redress of grievances.

But then came the European Convention on Human Rights adopted in 1950. Article 8 reads:

1. Everyone has the right to respect for his private and family life, his home and his correspondence.
2. There shall be no interference by a public authority with the exercise of this right except such as is in accordance with the law and is necessary in a democratic society in the interests of national security, public safety or the economic well-being of the country, for the prevention of disorder or crime, for the protection of health or morals, or for the protection of the rights and freedoms of others.

Already you can see how exceptions are creeping in and the broad categories under which state interference is now acceptable. This is the European bureaucrat rebranding himself from 'state as societal menace' to 'state as society's preserver and protector'.

After the Second World War, privacy laws were a means of protecting the individual from the state, because the greatest abuses of privacy, indeed of all human rights, were committed by government institutions and their accompanying bureaucracies. That's not to say individuals weren't involved in wrongdoing – there will always be criminals and murderers – but one person can only harm so many people. It takes a bureaucracy to violate human rights on an industrial scale.

In the UK, concern about privacy intrusion remains fixed solidly on our fellow citizens, projects such as Google Streetview and, most notably, the press. The strong, centralised state, in contrast, is seen as benevolent. History indicates the exact opposite is true: the less free the press, the more likely that tyranny can take hold. The more centralised and powerful the state, the greater the danger to the greatest number of individuals. So why do we continue to buy into the erroneous idea that we must be frightened of each other and only the state can save us?

It begins with the message. The message is pumped out relentlessly by those in power regardless of political party; it is peddled by all sorts of official organisations who hire huge cadres of press officers at our expense or buy in the services of corporate public relations firms (a process fully explored in Chapter 2). The message is constantly broadcast to the media and to the public in such a ubiquitous way that we no longer even notice how utterly false, insulting and anti-democratic it is. The message is this: *We, the people, cannot be trusted to manage our own affairs.*

Not only do we need the state to look after us but we are so God-awful that we cannot even be trusted to handle the simplest problem ourselves, whether that's telling off a child who is trampling a park flower bed or managing a village fete. Only the state can be trusted to keep our neighbourhoods free from thugs or our children in school. Rather than the state being seen as a threat, the threat is now us: our neighbours, our fellow citizens, the news media – basically anyone who does not work for or on behalf of the state.

The state is 'Big Daddy', looking out for us, protecting us. CCTV is there for 'our protection'. The huge databases growing within our local councils and quangos like cancers are there not to spy on us but to make our lives easier, richer, happier and more efficient. The most intrusive databases are being peddled under that great phrase of fascism, 'to protect the children'. The ultimate needle into the mainstream of reactionary emotionalism. This provides a shocking glimpse of the extent of the surveillance culture in twenty-first-century Britain.

Protecting the children

Here are just some of the systems in existence with the purported aim of 'protecting children'. By the time of publication there may be more.[1]

- **National Childhood Obesity Database** – the largest of its kind in the world, containing the height and weight of every pupil in Year 1 and Year 6 since 2005.
- **The National Pupil Database** – holds data on every pupil in state schools and state-funded nurseries and childcare, including information on name, age, address, ethnicity, special educational needs, free school-meal entitlement, whether the child is in care, behaviour and attendance records. This is to be shared with social workers, police and others.
- **ContactPoint** – a national index of all children in England that holds the biographical and contact information of children, along with notification of whether an in-depth assessment was done on the child and if so whether it is available to view. While

1. My thanks to the Foundation for Information Policy Research for their stellar work digging out this material for their report 'The Database State' from a stubbornly silent state (press releases are rarely issued on the creation of these databases).

details of services such as sexual or mental health will not generally be available there will be a note of 'unspecified sensitive service'. Local councils are responsible for shielding the records of vulnerable children (e.g. if they are escaping domestic violence). Initial set-up cost £224 million with annual running costs of £44 million annually from 2010/11 onwards.

- **Common Assessment Framework and eCAF** – a personal profiling tool through which children who need extra services or the state believes are not making progress towards the government's stated childhood 'targets' are assessed by 'personal advisers'. The forms are extensive and record not just facts but the subjective judgements of the adviser about the child and family members.

- **Integrated Children's System** – an electronic case-management system used by social workers, heavily weighted towards maximum data capture even to the point of social workers complaining it removes the focus from dealing with actual real-world situations and families. At the time of seventeen-month-old Baby P's death in August 2007, Haringey's social services were labelled 'good' largely as a result of the data collected on this system, which gives some indication of the gap between data and reality.

- **ASSET** – introduced in 2000 across the youth justice system in England and Wales. It includes assessments designed to profile young offenders by examining contributory factors that have brought them into the criminal justice system. The Young Offender Assessment Profile is used to prepare pre-sentence reports for the courts and includes much subjective judgement. Youth Offending Teams complete a 24-page Core Profile about education, family circumstances, living arrangements, lifestyle, substance abuse, physical and mental health, attitudes to offending and motivation to change. The profiler gives a score for each category which is then used to predict the likelihood of reoffending and make sentencing recommendations accordingly.

- **ONSET** – a Home Office system that gathers information and seeks to predict which children will offend in future. The six-page ONSET assessment form gathers information about contact with police and social services, family circumstances, educational history, lifestyle, substance abuse, physical and mental health, attitudes to offending and motivation to change.
- In addition, there about 39,000 children on the **National DNA** Database.

If that's the first time you've seen this list you might wonder why it's not more widely known or publicised. This is because the creation and expansion of these databases happens for the most part behind closed doors with little or no public input (but plenty of public money), as the following story reveals.

Terri Dowty is a motherly figure. She has grey hair, kindly eyes and a warm manner. She looks rather like a popular schoolteacher, probably because in her youth she worked as one. Twenty years ago she had her own children and became interested in children's rights. She's a natural as the director of Action on Rights for Children, a network of lawyers, academics, parents and young people interested in democratic forms of education and children's civil rights. The group started in 2001 to address concerns about a new style of school census and a new state database of teenagers' personal information.

'In 2000 we had a call from someone working in a local authority who'd been told she had to start supplying a whole load of personal information about kids aged thirteen to nineteen,' Terri told me. 'She was uncomfortable with some of the stuff she was supposed to collect. It was really personal and she couldn't see any good reason why that sort of stuff should be recorded. It was intrusive.'

Terri and her colleagues began investigating and the more they dug the more worried they became. They discovered the database was part of a government pilot scheme called 'Connexions', introduced by the Learning and Skills Act 2000, which included provisions for the widespread sharing of teenagers' personal data. They found that a new school census was also taking place and, rather than recording the numbers of special needs kids or those receiving free school meals, it gathered all sorts of personal data about individual pupils. Terri wondered how this could happen, because under section 537 of the Education Act 1996 the government was only allowed to collect school-level data and was expressly forbidden from recording individual pupil data. Yet here they were doing exactly that by taking pupils' data directly from school systems. After a bit of legislative digging, Terri and her team uncovered how two new databases had been slipped into existence with almost no public debate and certainly no public scrutiny. It's a story that is indicative of the way all government databases are created.

It began with amendments made to sections of bills passed in 1997 and 1998. These amendments changed the wording of the original Education Act so that instead of information being collected at *school* level it would be at *pupil* level. It was just one word but it made all the difference to the new state surveillance agenda. Then, as the bill was in the final Commons Committee, another amendment was sneaked in allowing the data to be shared across government. There was no full parliamentary debate and almost no debate in the committee about these radical changes.

'It seemed as though most MPs had no clue what was happening,' Terri told me. 'They weren't up to speed at all, so allowing such extensive powers to be given to the Secretary of State without debating them was outrageous.'

The actual data to be collected, it transpired, wasn't even specified in the legislation but was left up to the discretion of the Secretary of State for him or her to define in 'regulations', i.e. statutory instruments that don't require any debate in Parliament. Statutory instruments are intended to grant lawmakers an efficient way of implementing the nitty-gritty of an *existing* law, not to create new ones. But this new legislation gave the Secretary of State a blank cheque to prescribe the content and governance of children's databases in regulations. Only after Terri and others lobbied hard did politicians agree to specify what data items would be recorded. But even so, the law is such that at any time the Secretary of State can vary the data collected without consulting Parliament.

In the same manner that a frog put into a pot of cool water won't initially notice a gradual increase in temperature until it is too late, so the government introduced a series of statutory instruments that incrementally increased the range and quantity of data collected on children, so that there are now forty separate data items taken three times annually from children for the school census. These items are then fed into a **National Pupil Database.** And it doesn't stop there. Once the information is on one database it can be used to populate new ones. For example, the information from the National Pupil Database was initially used only for research, but is now being used to build up other state projects about which we are entirely ignorant.

Bad Connexions

Part of the reason we know so little about these systems is that they are incredibly slippery – not only are new ones created covertly, but the names of existing ones frequently change. Back in 1999, for example, the government's Social Exclusion Unit published a report called 'Bridging the Gap' that showed there were around 161,000 young people aged sixteen to eighteen who were not in education, employment or training. They were dubbed the 'Neets' and the government's response to this problem was the same as to any number of social problems of the past decade: build a database!

The first step was to replace the old careers advisers with 'personal advisers', whose remit went far beyond simply helping kids do well in exams or find a career. They were charged with overseeing every aspect of a child's life and then sharing that data with other agencies. Youths were targeted if they appeared 'disengaged' from education, but also if their circumstances matched the government's criteria for determining risk.

The stated aim of the Connexions database was to reduce Neets. And aside from the privacy implications, which were never discussed, who could argue with that? Alarmingly,

3| 2210670.

however, Connexions turned out to be merely a pilot for a much larger project: the **Every Child Matters agenda**, introduced in a Green Paper in 2003 and given life by the Children Act 2004. The idea was to extend the Connexions information-sharing approach to all children from birth. Every Child Matters was presented as a bold new idea, indeed as a response to the Laming Report into eight-year-old Victoria Climbié's death in 2000, but this was misleading. It was merely a rebrand of an existing policy known as **Identification, Referral and Tracking** which had existed before the Laming Inquiry even opened, and which had already morphed into something called **Information Sharing and Assessment**. The Every Child Matters Green Paper proposed a massive, central database containing the details of every child in England. Originally called the **Children's Index**, this was rebranded as **ContactPoint** in an attempt to quell the negative publicity surrounding the project. Confused yet?

ContactPoint is where we are today but doubtless there will be other name changes because the fact is the system doesn't work – the number of Neets has risen steadily since the state got involved. The Social Exclusion Unit that produced the report was shut down and the work transferred to the Cabinet Office's 'Social Exclusion Task Force'. Different name, same bureaucratic bullshit. It is envisaged that ContactPoint will store the details of every child from birth to age eighteen.

Every child watched

Many would argue that child protection is one of the state's most important and urgent roles. Ever since the death of

Maria Colwell in 1973, it's been an accepted principle that family information should be shared, with or without consent, when a child is at serious risk of harm from neglect or abuse. The problem now, however, isn't sharing information about serious cases of child abuse, but rather the state's new involvement in all aspects of childhood, since it is now monitoring *every youth* and not just for the risk of serious abuse.

Check out an extract from the Common Assessment Framework (CAF) form on the following pages to see just what a nosey parker the state has become. Almost a third of children in Britain are now assessed and profiled using the CAF form.

CAF assessment summary: strengths and needs

Consider each of the elements to the extent they are appropriate in the circumstances. You do not need to comment on every element. Wherever possible, base comments on evidence, not just opinion, and indicate what your evidence is. However, if there are any major differences of view, these should be recorded too.

1. Development of unborn baby, infant, child or young person

Health

General health
Conditions and impairments; access to and use of dentist, GP, optician; immunisations, developmental checks, hospital admissions, accidents, health advice and information

Physical development
Nourishment; activity; relaxation; vision and hearing; fine motor skills (drawing etc.); gross motor skills (mobility, playing games and sport etc.)

Speech, language and communication
Preferred communication, language, conversation, expression, questioning; games; stories and songs; listening; responding; understanding

Emotional and social development
Feeling special; early attachments; risking/actual self-harm; phobias; psychological difficulties; coping with stress; motivation, positive attitudes; confidence; relationships with peers; feeling isolated and solitary; fears; often unhappy

Behavioural development
Lifestyle, self-control, reckless or impulsive activity; behaviour with peers; substance misuse; anti-social behaviour; sexual behaviour; offending; violence and aggression; restless and overactive; easily distracted, attention span/concentration

1. Development of unborn baby, infant, child or young person (continued)

Identity, self-esteem, self-image and social presentation
Perceptions of self; knowledge of personal/family history; sense of belonging; experiences of discrimination due to race, religion, age, gender, sexuality and disability

Family and social relationships
Building stable relationships with family, peers and wider community; helping others; friendships; levels of association for negative relationships

Self-care skills and independence
Becoming independent; boundaries, rules, asking for help, decision-making; changes to body; washing, dressing, feeding; positive separation from family

Learning

Understanding, reasoning and problem solving
Organising, making connections; being creative, exploring, experimenting; imaginative play and interaction

Participation in learning, education and employment
Access and engagement; attendance, participation; adult support; access to appropriate resources

Progress and achievement in learning
Progress in basic and key skills; available opportunities; support with disruption to education; level of adult interest

Aspirations
Ambition; pupil's confidence and view of progress; motivation, perseverance

The assessment is meant to be a voluntary process done with consent, but in practice it's very difficult (and impossible in many areas of England) for families to access state services without agreeing to it. Also, the state has arbitrarily decided that children of twelve and older can give their own consent even if the law says otherwise.

The government's own commissioned research of the assessment forms found practitioners weren't keen on them. Some complained this was due to the lack of training: 'Two hours on a training course wasn't nearly enough.' Another thought the form was 'too intrusive', while others believed it was impractical for all but the most serious abuse cases. Rather than listening to the people on the ground who actually have to deal with families, the project was rolled out regardless across the nation.

On the form you'll see many of the factors are entirely subjective, based on the judgement of the assessor (any practitioner who knows the child, be they childminder, teacher or psychotherapist). They might only 'know' them in terms of meeting them just once, but because they are agents of the all-powerful state, they sit and score the child and her family. Would any of us like to be judged in this manner? The government line is that such nosiness ensures that children achieve the set of 'outcomes' defined by the government in Every Child Matters, but why should the state be allowed to do this? It has now set itself up to be nothing less than a 'partner' in parenting, obsessively identifying 'targets' and defining the proper way to raise a child. Guidance entitled 'Every Parent Matters' says as much: 'The role of government is to ensure that all parents ... work in partnership with services to reinforce the benefits for their children's outcomes.'

It is the state, of course, defining these outcomes, not parents. Schools are no longer simply for learning, but are becoming factories of social engineering. Parents haven't been asked their views on the state's new self-selected role as parenting partner, nor have children expressed any wish to have responsibility for their upbringing shared between their parents and government. How on earth has it come to this?

The answer lies in Lisbon, March 2002, at a meeting of European Union heads of state in which they discussed ways of harnessing the power of information technology. There was widespread agreement that the struggling IT industry which had just suffered the dot.com bust could be subsidised by states keen to expand their power. Each EU country was to develop its service delivery by electronic means or 'e-government', the stated aim to offer citizens faster, more efficient services, while also stimulating the IT market.[2] In Britain, the Cabinet Office's Performance and Innovation Unit was charged with implementing 'e-government' and in April 2002 produced a report, 'Privacy and Data-sharing', identifying areas where the government could make rapid progress. One of those areas was the collection of data on children, young people and their families who might need public services. The creation of such a database was hugely controversial, however, and those in Whitehall knew it would be a

2. The unstated aim was to maximise revenue by selling information back to the public, something we'll explore in Chapter 5.

hard sell to the public unless they could present it in an acceptable way.

During this time Terri and her colleagues were awaiting a long overdue Green Paper on reforming child protection. The service needed a dramatic overhaul and yet the government kept putting off change. Then Victoria Climbié died and child protection hit the headlines, the pressure mounted on ministers and in November 2003 the government announced the 'Every Child Matters' policy.

'It was dressed up as child protection but it wasn't at all,' Terri says. 'It was the most shameless piece of shroud waving I've seen.'

Actual 'child protection' relates to about 50,000 children in the UK who are believed to be 'at substantial risk of significant harm'. That's already too much for social services to handle, given the perennial, chronic shortage of specialised social workers. But rather than sorting out the child protection system, the state expanded its remit into all forms of 'child welfare' and the focus switched to another 3–4 million children who simply need services, flooding an already stretched system with low-level information that threatened to drown out the voices of children who are actually in danger.

When data becomes dangerous

Maria Ward had eighteen different cases on her books when Baby P died, 50 per cent more than the council's own limit of twelve cases per social worker. Ward was one of many social workers, health visitors and doctors who saw Baby P sixty times in the eight months leading up to his death but failed to intervene. Victoria Climbié's social worker Lisa Arthurworrey was overstretched with nineteen cases.

A decade on from the Climbié inquiry, all indications are that child protection services are getting steadily worse. Laying aside the civil liberties issues of intrusive databases and profiling children, the main objections to universal surveillance must be effectiveness and cost. It takes a huge amount of cash to keep tabs on every single child in the country. Money that could be spent recruiting and training social workers.

An Ofsted report in December 2008 found the number of councils failing to keep children safe had doubled in the past year and these reports are far from scathing. They are not based on surprise inspections but rather data supplied by the councils themselves so there is ample opportunity for painting a prettier picture than reality. The Ofsted annual report of 2008 assessed 150 local authorities in England. While 73 per cent were judged to be good or outstanding, that was fewer than the 78 per cent the previous year. Another report done by the Audit Commission in 2009 revealed the performance ratings of more than one in five councils had declined since 2005, with a quarter of councils providing inadequate or minimal services for young people. The commission concluded that England's 150 children's services departments 'performed slightly worse in 2008 than in 2005', a period in which the ratings of council services such as housing, waste disposal and care of older people had consistently improved.

To most of us with common sense the reason for the decline is obvious: too much bureaucracy and too little accountability to the public. Lord Laming's report into Baby P's death condemned the 'over-complicated, lengthy and tickbox assessment and recording system' that developed after his earlier Climbié report as a result of a raft of Whitehall 'reforms'. With so much information to record, social workers 'often do not have the time needed to maintain effective contact with children'.

You know things are bad when even the bureaucrats are protesting against 'excessive bureaucracy' as social workers complained to the Children and Family Court Advisory and Support Service. 'Many Cafcass staff who have recently left local authority practice referred to the flaws of the children's social care Integrated Children's System [ICS].' Adding, 'Particular concerns hinge around the combined demands of computer systems which many practitioners experience as over-controlling and channelling their thinking into the processes and data required by their organisations, in the process disrupting the reflective practice needed in the most complex family cases.'

The irony is that if the state actually listened to ordinary people, instead of relying on such cumbersome and unreliable systems, it would often know a lot more about what's going on. Take the practice of profiling children for the purpose of spotting which children will become delinquent or socially excluded. There are countless problems with profiling: its effectiveness is disputed;[3] its ethics are

3. Britain's most eminent criminologist, Professor David Farrington, has said that 'any notion that better screening can enable policymakers to identify young children destined to join the 5 per cent of offenders responsible for 50–60 per cent of crime is fanciful'. However, the government points to an evaluation carried out by Oxford University's

dubious; and there is also the danger that the related ONSET profiling, which deals with children who have not actually committed a criminal offence, becomes a self-fulfilling prophecy so that a perfectly law-abiding youngster from a poor home with learning and health difficulties and thus flagged as a 'potential offender' would find he gets much less attention from teachers and much more from local police, which could then lead him to becoming an offender.

Most worryingly, though – and despite the lengthy assessment forms – the profiles are simply a snapshot in time. Might not a better assessment be made by an ordinary person who lives next to the youth or someone who has been assaulted? It is here that we see the state's disdain and distrust of the common person.

Look at the case of two brothers in Edlington, South Yorkshire, who tortured and assaulted a nine-year-old boy and his eleven-year-old uncle in April 2009, leaving them for dead. The brothers' 36-year-old divorced mother had seven sons from two relationships, one of whom had already been sent to a young offender institution the same year for mugging an old woman. By the front door of the family's home a sign read: 'Beware of the Kids'.

Neighbours told *The Times* newspaper that the children went from throwing eggs at their house to smashing their

---

Centre for Criminological Research (the designers of ASSET) in August 2005 which found that ASSET scores *could* predict reconviction within two years with 69.4 per cent accuracy. But when the Foundation for Policy Information Research tried to examine the basis for these statistics they were not convinced.

windows with stones and then to drawing blood by hurling rocks at a mother and her three-year-old son. The two brothers targeted an Iraqi Kurd family who lived next door. They threw fruit, paint, dog food, water balloons, half-eaten burgers, a gas cylinder, bottles, pebbles and gravel – at the house, at the car, into the garden and at the family themselves. The father complained to the boys' mother who ignored him. He sought help from the police and council. Police officers and police community support officers went to the house five times in response to incidents but no action was taken. The neighbours had visits from the council's 'safer neighbourhood team' and two joint meetings were held but again no action was taken.

Eventually the police asked the family to stop contacting them after every attack. The father said: 'One officer said to me I should only contact them after every six or seven incidents. A council worker told us to write down everything that happened.'

It wasn't lack of information that led the Edlington brothers to become offenders. It was lack of response by the police and social workers to very real human intelligence – a consistent and recurring problem in a system where the only people who can take action are those sanctioned by the state. The rest of us are stripped of any rights to police our own streets and every criminal knows that. If we do try and enforce a code of behaviour then it is *us*, not the criminals, whom the officials will punish – and even state workers face retaliation when they challenge the status quo that bureaucracy knows best.

Nevres Kemal was a social worker in Haringey who had serious concerns about the failings in the borough's social services department, which she described as 'out of control'. Six months before the death of Baby P she wrote to Patricia Hewitt (Health Secretary at the time) and three other ministers warning of a repeat of the Victoria Climbié tragedy. In response, the council not only dismissed Kemal but took out an injunction banning her from speaking about childcare in Haringey, and because of a confidentiality agreement (now a mandatory part of many public servants' contracts) she had to fight even to speak freely at the public inquiry into Baby P's death.

What all of this shows is that a plethora of data doesn't make us safer nor equal good-quality services. As long as officials are accountable only to Whitehall and other bureaucrats rather than directly to the public, the incentives are geared towards creating Soviet-style tractor targets, not satisfying the citizen or solving civic problems.

When the state controls everything and takes over every aspect of our lives even to the point of becoming a 'partner in parenting', the people are paralysed by powerlessness. Assessing the 'identity and self-image' or 'life skills' of children isn't the role of the state, at least not until it's got a handle on protecting children from serious abuse (which it clearly hasn't). In a free society the family is sacrosanct. The state only intervenes where there is a risk of harm or negligence to a child. When you start talking about state involvement to 'prevent' bad things from happening then you're giving the state the power to intervene when *nothing* has gone wrong. It's a fanciful idea that a bureaucrat can predict which child will become a criminal: our criminal justice system isn't capable of dealing with real criminals, let alone foreseeing future ones. Instead, the focus of all this data-collecting falls on the vast majority of law-abiding citizens who have done nothing wrong. They are the easy targets.

The onward march of intrusive data collection goes on.

Your data doppelgänger

I want to end this chapter with one final warning: once the state takes over your identity, the onus is on you to prove you are who you say you are.

Rupert Collins-White, an editor of the *Law Society Gazette*, found himself in just such a catch-22 position when he discovered his local council (Haringey again) had recorded his name incorrectly on their official database. In a scene reminiscent of the film *Brazil*, a bureaucratic error led Rupert Collins-White to become for a year Rupert Colling-White. Movie buffs may recall that in *Brazil* a swatted fly led to the incarceration and execution of Mr Archibald Buttle instead of the suspected terrorist, Archibald Tuttle. When an upstairs neighbour tried to help the grieving wife of Mr Buttle she wound up being labelled a terrorist herself as the bureaucrats had no truck with the idea they had made a mistake.

Rupert discovered the error when he accessed his own credit report and found that for an entire year he had stopped existing and in his place was someone else: Rupert Colling-White. When he called the credit reference agency to report the error they told him they couldn't change the file because officially Rupert Colling-White *did* exist – he'd paid council tax and was on the electoral register of Haringey Council – and if Rupert had a problem with that he'd have to take it up with the council. Which he did.

'Essentially, I was told that my name had been entered incorrectly on the council tax system but that, because it wasn't the current year's data, it had been archived and couldn't be changed. "But that's my data, and it's wrong," said I. "It's on my credit record and makes out I have an alias and a lack of existence for a whole year." "Nothing we can do about that, I'm afraid," says the council. Their argument was that because that's what they had on file that was the "official" me regardless of who I actually I am.'

After the council's refusal to delete his alias, he phoned the credit reference agencies again who said they would flag his report indicating the situation, though it's unclear if that will give Rupert a clean credit rating.

'It makes you feel completely impotent – mostly because the council, the bureaucrats, just so obviously didn't care. They couldn't give a monkey's. It was what *they* called me that counted. Who I actually was, was irrelevant.'

Such incidents will become more common as the state takes over defining who we are.

In secrecy, bureaucracies grow large, ungainly and unaccountable to those they are meant to serve. When there is no fierce spotlight of public accountability shining, there is no pressure to ensure systems are streamlined or even working. What you find throughout any bureaucracy protected by secrecy is a cesspit of illogic and waste. And because the state keeps rebranding, shifting responsibility from one set of bureaucrats to another, most of the work being done is for the purpose of keeping other bureaucrats in employment rather than satisfying the needs of the public.

We now have some idea what the state knows about us – private citizens going about our private business – but what about public officials providing a public service with public money? Here we enter into the strangely Kafkaesque world where institutional privacy is protected at all costs, even while individual privacy is under assault.

Welcome now to the world of the silent state . . .

2

Spin and the Government's PR Machine

It's not totally correct to say the state is silent. It has plenty to say, it's just that most of what it says is nothing we want, or need, to hear. It is public relations, PR, spin – all polite terms for what is essentially taxpayer-subsidised propaganda.

In some ways it might be better if the state *were* silent – then at least we'd know how little we know that's of any importance. As it is, we're bamboozled by a bevy of free sheets, press releases masquerading as 'news' and pseudo-events. Just like the lawyer in the musical *Chicago*, the state uses PR to 'razzle-dazzle' us so we buy into flawed ideas, poor government and pseudo-democracy, all sold to us with the hype of a summer movie. And, just like most summer movies, the actual result is not very good. In the age of PR what's important is *selling* a product; whether that product is actually any good is irrelevant.

The products a government peddles are ideas, decisions, policies. They're sold to the public by the powerful using the techniques of corporate public relations. Officials hire internal or external PRs to manage public opinion and do policy placement – that is, putting a positive spin on a political policy or decision so the public believes it is a success. Such successes make officials look good and if they look good they'll remain in power and usually amass more. So what if the idea stinks? In the age of PR there is no such thing as failure. The underlying belief is that you *can* make shit smell like roses. This is the emperor's new clothes on a grand scale.

Public relations is at best promotion or the manipulation of facts; at worst it is evasion and outright deception. You can have soft spin (highlighting one fact above another) or hardcore propaganda (lies or smears), but PR is never about the free flow of information. It's not about solving civic problems either and has about as much right to be a part of democratic life as a ducking pool in a courtroom.

It would be a lie, though, to say PR isn't effective. It's effective in moulding public opinion in the short term for the benefit of a few elites. It's not effective for a long-term reputation nor for the health of society as a whole. And it's downright devastating for democracy.

This was brought home to me soon after I first moved to London. Working as a publicist for the BBC, I was having a great time – going to lots of parties, meeting lots of people and doing an inordinate amount of schmoozing. As a day job, writing press releases and pamphlets to sell television shows to overseas territories was a nice break from covering crime and politics on a daily basis, which is what I'd done before. Then I had some problems in my neighbourhood. Nothing wildly uncommon unfortunately: young thugs terrorising the community, the police doing nothing, the council completely impotent – and I wanted to find out why these bureaucrats were so useless. So I went to council meetings and tried to find out information.

It was at that point I discovered that in Britain the citizens' involvement ends the day after an election. Certainly there's no comprehension that I had any right to know the nitty-gritty of how my taxes were being spent. I was left feeling frustrated, angry and disempowered. I certainly wasn't getting any facts from the Tower Hamlets taxpayer-subsidised propaganda sheet *East End Life*. There was no detail in there about how many police officers worked a shift or how many incidents of assault happened on my street. All I got in that full-colour newspaper was a load of happy smiling cops and councillors telling me what a fine job they were doing and how lucky I was to be living in such a multicultural, vibrant community. I tried to remember this the next time I saw someone using the local park as a toilet (the actual public toilet having been closed by the council, probably to pay for the latest issue of *East End Life*). It was clear where the council placed its priorities. Listening to the public and responding to their actual concerns was of far less importance then telling us what they wanted us to know. This is the central principle of information control: one official opinion peddled through one official source. No other opinions are allowed, even if – especially if – you work for the state.

Inconvenient truths

Philip Balmforth was a former police inspector and vulnerable persons officer responsible for Asian women in the

Bradford area of West Yorkshire. He was praised in a House of Commons early day motion signed by fifty-six MPs in March 2008 for being a 'knight in shining armour' who 'does everything he can to protect people and give them time to assess the situation they are in'. A leading campaigner against forced marriage said he was 'the most experienced and effective police officer in the country in dealing with these issues'. Yet a week after he was praised in Parliament he was facing a disciplinary hearing for 'damaging the reputation' of West Yorkshire Police. What happened?

PR is what happened.

Balmforth was punished for having the audacity to speak directly to the public and not via the police press office. He dared to shine a light on an inconvenient truth: that some Asian families were kidnapping their daughters and forcing them into unwanted marriages. Bradford City councilmen said it was 'bad for regeneration', and they appear to have been willing to sacrifice young girls' lives so as not to offend their political power base.

'The Asian vote is a massive thing,' says Jasvinder Sanghera, co-founder of Karma Nirvana, a community-based project that supports South Asian women affected by domestic violence and honour-based crimes. 'Philip took action when the majority of people were afraid to do so. Most officials don't want to engage with this work for fear of being called racist. I've tried to get posters put up in schools and the head teachers will say they can't because they don't want to cause offence. So girls go missing and they are just written off. We know forced marriage happens across a number of communities, but the figures tell us they are predominantly South Asian, so let's not get all PC about things. It doesn't help.'

Forced marriage isn't an issue of cultural understanding. It's an abuse of one human by another. State officials who should be protecting the rights of vulnerable young girls are instead protecting the position of power held by men. Philip Balmforth is a national expert on forced marriage and his views have been sought by politicians, campaigners and members of the public including the press. Until he spoke out, the official line from councils, police and politicians was that forced marriage was not much of a problem. Balmforth gave a dissenting view. He challenged the figure given by the government that only three hundred cases of forced marriage were reported annually to the government's Forced Marriage Unit, saying he dealt with that many in West Yorkshire alone. Referring to the thirty-three girls missing in Bradford, he told *The Times*: 'If these girls are missing, who has been told? Who is doing anything about it? I want to know from every education authority, "How many children did you lose last year? And where are they?" At the moment, we just don't know. It's like knocking a nail into a piece of stone.'

It was largely as a result of Balmforth's informed opinion that ministers finally took action. They embarked on a project to try and trace missing girls in fifteen areas identified as forced-marriage risk zones. It was the first attempt to map the national scale of the problem.

We should be grateful to Balmforth for alerting us to this problem and helping to solve it by suggesting action. Yet that's not how Bradford City councillors saw it. After the piece appeared in the *Times* newspaper, senior officials claimed that Balmforth's high-profile work was damaging the city's image. They complained to his police force to the point that the force called him in for a disciplinary hearing.

When I phoned up the force press office at that time to ask how they could justify such a hearing, they at first tried to deny Balmforth was being punished for speaking out. But I'd been read the letter sent by the force and challenged the press officer with this, who then told me: 'It's not in Philip Balmforth's role to talk about those issues. Just as all officers are allocated to specific portfolios and to give comment on those.' They tried to claim Balmforth had not been disciplined but simply moved as a result of 'restructuring'.

At the time of writing, Balmforth still works at West Yorkshire Police but he's been totally removed from his area of expertise and I couldn't speak to him directly because he's forbidden from any communication with the public. He has been successfully silenced under the banner of maintaining the 'reputation' of West Yorkshire Police and Bradford City Council. I can't see how such egregious censorship is in any way good for the long-term health of either of these institutions not to mention the public. Forced marriage remains a problem. It won't just go away; bringing it to the public's attention is a first step towards addressing it. Preventing this from happening is a victory for those who kidnap women and force them into lives of systemic rape and enslavement.

What sort of message does an institution send out when it punishes qualified professionals for speaking the truth? Sanghera says she's had scores of emails from people saved or helped by Balmforth expressing utter disillusionment at the actions of the force.

The sad fact is that across the UK there are many Philip Balmforths – good people prepared to speak the truth to make public services the best they can be, yet they are silenced for the sake of so-called 'reputation management'.

Police PR

Philip Balmforth's story is part of a wider shift in the way the police operate. Simply put, the police are no longer there merely to deal with crime and keep us safe: they have a reputation to manage. The days when a police officer was concerned with 'just the facts' are long gone. West Yorkshire is just one of over fifty police forces in the UK, each of which now has a dedicated press office. Police forces are spending almost £40 million a year on spin doctors and news management. At a time when police budgets are under pressure and some forces are even facing budget capping, overall spending on PR in 2008 was up 13 per cent from two years earlier. You could put an extra 1,400 officers on the streets for the amount we spend subsidising police public relations.

Police force spending on marketing and PR increased when the Home Office changed the way it judged police performance from actual crime to the public's *perceptions* of crime. Police forces are now on a mission to 'reassure the public' through PR and it's not cheap. Scotland Yard, with a PR bill of more than £6 million, is the biggest spender. The danger of focusing so much on image is that it creates a perverse incentive to suppress or spin crime information, so that in the name of improving public confidence police forces are loath to put out yellow incident boards, for example, calling for witnesses. Two people might be murdered in their homes with more than a hundred horrific injuries, but the first line in a press release will be that the city is a safe place to work and live.

Creating this sort of *Alice in Wonderland* fairy tale neither solves crime nor makes us safer, because as long as the police are concentrating on PR they're not actually dealing with the root source of crime – criminals. If we don't know what crime is happening around us then we're less able to help the police with inquiries or offer tips and local knowledge ('human intelligence') which are essential for any good investigation. A more effective tool for building trust and a long-term reputation would be for the police to provide all criminal incident data in a timely, detailed and consistent way so that we could accurately assess the situation.

Yet that's exactly what we're not getting.

Nigel Green has spent the last ten years trying to get criminal incident data out of his local force in Northumbria. He's been reporting on crime for the past twenty-five years for various media outlets and now runs a local news agency. During his career he's seen a dramatic drop in the level of information made public by the police. A drop of inverse relation to the rise in press officers. Northumbria Police increased its PR spend by 55 per cent in the two years up to 2008 and by 2009 it was spending nearly £1.5 million.

Green examined one month's worth of press releases issued by the force for a thesis at Newcastle University and found that, on average, it takes one week for the police to release details of a crime. In the old days, reporters used to speak directly to detective inspectors and they'd get detailed facts about crimes within a day. 'I've written three historic crime books and I find it ironic that journalists in the nineteenth century got far more information, far more quickly, than they do in the twenty-first century.'

He was also shocked to find just how much *churnalism* was practised, whereby journalists rewrite police press releases instead of doing real reporting. 'All we get are stories about how crime is falling and how they're doing such a great job,' he said. As if that's not bad enough, local newspapers are so under-resourced now that they just print releases almost verbatim.

Manufacturing reality

In the public sphere, perception is reality: it's more important to be *seen* to do something than actually to do it. At least when private companies use PR and advertising they must spend their own money and there are other corporations vying for our business. If a company doesn't give us what we want they face bankruptcy. Public institutions, however, are monopolies. We have no choice but to buy, if not use, their services. If we don't like the way our particular police force operates it's not like we can choose another one or even withhold the money used to run the one we don't like. We're forced – under threat of imprisonment – to pay for a monopoly service and for it to tell us how great it is.

This is the real danger of institutional PR. In the absence

of competition it is only through a diversity of opinion and public scrutiny that some level of accountability can exist. PR stifles debate and suppresses opinion through the use of centralised press offices and communication protocols.

The best PR is invisible, like senior civil servants, so it's hard to know the full extent of its takeover of our public services. Officials know we don't like seeing our taxes spent on this sort of propaganda so they're keen to find ways of hiding it by taking it off the account books. But I've spent the past five years digging around in this area, and here's a glimpse of what I've found.

Local government propaganda

In the absence of civic investigative journalism, the campaign group for lower taxes, the TaxPayers' Alliance (TPA), has done the most work to investigate local council spending on publicity. Researchers looked at the annual reports of hundreds of local councils where a separate listing must be made of PR and publicity spending. You won't find any press releases pouring forth about this newsworthy figure. Instead, the TPA's researchers had to trawl through 445 annual reports just for 2008 and then all those again for previous years to compare spending. Many councils complained bitterly when the TaxPayers' Alliance report came out, but as the figures are the councils' own there's not a lot they can do to smear the source of this unsanctioned information – though they give it a go.

The 2008 report revealed the average local authority spent almost £1 million (£971,985) on publicity.

- The total local authority publicity bill is now over £430 million.
- The average local authority is spending twice the amount on publicity than it did in 1996–97:
  - in 1996–97, the average local authority spent £429,887 on publicity;
  - in 2006–7, the average local authority spent £954,023 on publicity;
  - in 2007–8, the average local authority spent £971,985 on publicity.
- There are six local authorities spending more than £5 million on publicity.
- At least 225 councils have increased their spending on publicity since the 2006–7 financial year.
- The twenty councils spending the most money on publicity accumulated a bill of more than £100 million.
- There is one local authority, Birmingham City Council, that spent more than £9 million on publicity.
- However, at least 217 councils have decreased spending on publicity, collectively cutting over £25 million from their budgets and proving that councils can reduce unnecessary spending.

And remember Tower Hamlets, my old council and one of Britain's most deprived boroughs? They spent £2,354,000 in 2007–8 on press and PR – an increase of 82.6 per cent from ten years before.

	Spending on publicity, £			% increase
Council	1996–7	2006–7	2007–8	1996–7 to 2007–8
Birmingham	6,900,000	10,400,000	9,200,000	33%
Liverpool	1,158,000	9,402,000	7,540,000	551%
Surrey	-	5,100,000	6,200,000	-
Bradford	907,000	5,606,000	6,016,000	563%
Kent	1,409,000	6,586,000	5,683,000	303%
Manchester	2,283,742	5,226,000	5,118,000	124%
Sunderland	-	4,376,815	4,926,854	-
Southwark	1,454,026	5,057,000	4,776,000	229%
Essex	2,455,000	4,332,000	4,775,000	95%
Lincolnshire	1,176,121	3,733,865	4,716,121	301%

If you were hoping your local newspaper was looking into council spending, I have some bad news. Local papers are closing at a record rate and while there were about 1,300 local newspapers in Britain in 2009 very few have the resources to practise 'journalism of verification' – that is, finding, analysing and verifying official information and making it meaningful and comprehensible to the general public. This sort of journalism is expensive and very few media outlets are interested in funding it due to the cost. Added to that is a woeful libel law and a perceived opinion held by many editors that the public just aren't interested. I think the MPs' expenses scandal shows that's not the case.

It doesn't cost the $3 million spent by the *New York Times* on their Baghdad bureau to cover a local hospital or council, but for most local media it's money they no longer have. The same cannot be said for the local councils.

Sixty-six per cent of councils produce a magazine and 28 per cent produce a newspaper, while only 6 per cent produce neither, according to a survey conducted between October 2008 and April 2009 by LG Communications.

Lincup, NewsWyre, Hartbeat – they usually have a playful pun in the name, but there is nothing funny about propaganda paid for by the public that stops the public finding out how public money is spent. And it's even more Kafkaesque: without the least shame, these wasteful councils even have the gall to fill their pseudo-newspapers with puff pieces about how cost-efficient they are! In the survey mentioned above, in answer to the question 'Which topics are likely to get most coverage in your magazine/newspaper?', the third most popular answer, at 52 per cent, was 'How the council provides value for money'. This was topped only by recycling (74 per cent) and crime and antisocial behaviour (53 per cent).

These pravda rags are a relatively recent phenomenon: 88 per cent have come into existence since the 1990s. Across London, official council newspapers now employ around 120 people. When council press officers, who write most of the articles in the papers, are included, the figure rises to 360. The total number of editorial staff on all independent local newspapers in London at that time was 350. (According to the book *The British Press*, between 1985 and 2005, 401 regional and local papers – nearly one-quarter of all titles – closed down. Those that survived were hit with massive circulation drops. For example, the *Birmingham Evening Mail* has lost 54 per cent of its circulation since 1995 and the *Sheffield Star* 38 per cent. More than half of the 8,000 journalists in the provinces lost their jobs between 1986 and 2000.)

Let's take a look at *East End Life*, the newspaper of my former council Tower Hamlets. It runs to seventy-two pages – nearly double the size of the independent newspaper the *East London Advertiser*, and with almost 50 per cent more staff. In his investigation published in the *Evening Standard*, Andrew Gilligan examined the council's claim that the newspaper cost taxpayers just £118,000 a year. They claimed the rest of the £1.56 million cost was covered by advertising. But what they didn't say, and what Gilligan discovered when he looked at all those ads, was that the bulk were paid for by other public bodies such as the NHS or police. Gilligan estimated that public sector organisations paid a total of £980,000 to advertise in *East End Life*, making its true cost to the public purse much higher.

'The council wants a complete monopoly of the news in Tower Hamlets,' *Advertiser* editor Malcolm Starbrook told Gilligan. He related how his staff had been barred from the last election count and how council press releases were issued too late for inclusion in the paper. Gilligan got hold of a copy of a presentation given by Tower Hamlets' head of commercial operations (at that time Chris Payne) where he set out the council's rationale: independent local papers, he said, 'churn out a negative diet of crime and grime, often attacking their local council and generally creating a negative impression'. Council papers, by contrast, 'help create a positive place-shaping agenda, talking up an area and its residents' achievements, celebrating diversity and opportunity for all'.

Gilligan then took apart the coverage of one issue of *East End Life* and found the names of councillors mentioned twenty-seven times, including six mentions of the same councillor, with photographs of twelve of them. Good news predominated while scandals were ignored. In February, the pseudo-paper claimed Tower Hamlets' 2009/10 council tax rise was 'among the lowest in London' when according to the government's own figures, it was in fact the fifteenth highest out of thirty-three boroughs.

What you'll never see in any council publicity is a full-page notice telling the public about their most powerful right of access – the Audit Commission Act 1998. This law allows local taxpayers full rein to pile through all the council's accounts and accompanying audit documents for twenty full working days. You want to see the details of a dodgy contract? All of a councillor's expense receipts? Hotel bills? The chief exec's corporate credit card bill? It's all here for twenty days only. You can inspect all books, deeds, contracts, bills, vouchers and receipts relating to the audit. You can also make copies of any of these documents. The chances of finding this advertised prominently by any council is about as likely as a parking attendant ripping up a ticket. Local councils even have a statutory duty to advertise the inspection period but they do so in one newspaper in the smallest possible ad and if you miss it you won't find it anywhere else.

My prediction is this: the more officials take over the news the more corruption will sweep across government and the more our money will be wasted. It is scrutiny by the general public that keeps the powerful honest. Not other bureaucrats, not other politicians, not regulators – there is only one interest group that can never be captured in totality and that is the general public.

Some councils are starting to see sense. In August 2009,

Lancashire County Council was saving nearly £300,000 by cutting back its *Vision* magazine from ten to two editions annually. But this is just one island of sense in a rising sea of spin.

Central government propaganda

Central government spending on propaganda isn't new. The Central Office of Information was created in 1946 from the former Ministry of Information. It had its critics from the beginning such as MP Rupert De la Bère who complained in 1949 that the COI had 'never ceased to offend by wasting and squandering public money, and is it not high time that the use of this service for government propaganda should cease in an endeavour to get rid of this tied house? Let us be quite frank about it.'

The COI's mission statement is 'to use its communications expertise to help government achieve policy objectives'. It's certainly been doing a lot of that. Spending by the COI increased by 43 per cent to £540 million in 2008/9, making it the country's biggest single advertiser, according to Nielsen. The British government even outspent Procter & Gamble and its nearest competitor in ad revenue terms by £38m for the twelve months to March 2009.

Costs are even higher when the PR spending of departments and the thousands of executive agencies and quangos are included. Unlike local councils, however, these public bodies have no statutory obligation to keep a separate record of their publicity spending, so the only way to uncover that detail is to make freedom-of-information requests (which is where the majority of the evidence in this chapter comes from). The absolute lowest amount spent on press and PR across thirteen Whitehall departments was £27.6 million a year for a staff of 709 PR and communications officers. This figure is wildly deceptive, however, as many departments failed to provide the costs of contracting out PR work to outside agencies or the production costs of various newsletters. Many of the high-profile behaviour change campaigns, for example, are handled by private agencies such as Kindred and Trimedia.

When I asked for a detailed breakdown of spending I saw the discrepancy. Suddenly the costs rose from £19.6 million (for the seven departments which provided a breakdown) to £148.1 million for just one year. The Department for Environment, Food and Rural Affairs (DEFRA) initially told me it spent just £2,500 per year on newsletters but when pressed suddenly found the cost to be £130,000.

Did I mention how utterly unhelpful bureaucrats are when it comes to telling the public important information – like where our money goes? Several departments claimed they couldn't compile the figures because telling the public how public money is spent would be too expensive. This is funny because they actually provided much of the information to a Lords select committee report on communications back in December 2008. One of the more egregious disparities I found comparing the two sets of answers involved the Department of Health, which claimed just fifty-four communications staff were employed while in the Lords select committee report they admit to employing 122.

Foreign and Commonwealth Office

The cost of the press operation at the Foreign and Commonwealth Office in London, which employs thirty staff, is £11.5 million. There are a further seventy staff in London employed directly on communications-related activity (such as website work, events, publications). There are also about 390 staff doing communications work in UK missions overseas. The total budget for which the Strategic Communications Director has managerial responsibility is £497 million, but this includes the FCO's funding of the BBC World Service, the British Council, Wilton Park and scholarship programmes. And the FCO also has its own publication – a monthly magazine called *News and Views* which cost the public £162,307 in 2009 but which is only available internally.

Ministry of Defence

The Directorate General of Media and Communications in the MoD had 184 staff and a budget of £15.6 million in 2007/8 (up from £14.9 million in 2006/7). There are a further 157 staff in the MoD whose primary work is communications. This includes staff in the Meteorological Office, the Estates Organisation and the Equipment and Support Organisation. The MoD estimates the expenditure associated with these other staff at about a further £15 million, though this does not include direct manpower costs. The three armed services also have staff engaged in communications work (for example, public relations officers in regiments and on ships) and make use of PR agencies. The main PR expenditure in 2007/8 by the armed services on nationally organised campaigns and events, including recruitment campaigns, was over £44 million. Of this, the largest expenditure was by the army, at £24.3 million. The MoD claimed it would be too costly to tell the public how much public money is spent on its self-congratulatory magazines (as there are quite a number apparently). But I did manage to prise from them details of production costs (excluding staff) of the main MoD publication, *Defence Focus* – £187,000 in 2009.

Department of Health

The DoH had 122 staff engaged in communications work in 2007/8 of whom thirty were press officers. The total budget for the communications division of DoH was £52.2 million. This was made up of an administrative budget of £7.1 million covering the cost of the 122 staff and their day-to-day operations, and £45.1 million of programme costs. In 2008/9 the total budget allocation rose to £107 million. The administrative budget rose by 7 per cent to £7.6 million, while the programme costs more than doubled to £99.6 million. The main reasons for the large increase in the programme costs were the launch of a major campaign on obesity and a significant increase in expenditure on tobacco control.

Bear in mind these figures are only what the DoH hasn't managed to hide. A good heaping of health publicity is done by outside PR agencies such as Fishburn Hedges, Porter Novelli, Good Relations (and its parent Bell Pottinger). Also, the official figures don't seem to include sums spent on self-promotion (some might say aggrandisement) which includes films/DVDs on the National Programme for IT (there's even a board game devised to get buy-in on the disastrous IT project), promotional leaflets, roadshows involving hotel and venue bookings, and even independent reports which are not published until the Department of Health likes what is said. In relation to the DoH's propaganda papers I received this very unhelpful reply: 'I can confirm that the Department operates two internal newsletters – "Hugh Taylor's Update" and the "Managers' Briefing". However, to extract this information, calculating the cost of authorship, editing, and related costs over the past three years ... would exceed the appropriate limit.' No private publisher could operate without a budget this way, and note the sudden prudence when it comes to informing the public!

At a wider government level, it's also interesting to compare the number of communication officers (telling us what the government wants us to know – the official line) with the number of freedom-of-information officers (responding to what we actually want to know). My research reveals that government departments continue to hire on average twelve communications officers for each FOI person (at the Department for International Development that figure was twenty-five to one) and spend £10 on communications for each £1 spent on FOI. And when departments included their agency costs that figure jumps to £75 for every £1 spent on FOI.

It's plain that the public sector is now a big part of any PR agency's business. Chime Communications, the PR and marketing agency run by Lord Bell, a former adviser to

Margaret Thatcher, reported in March 2009 that its full-year pre-tax profits had risen by 19 per cent to £16.3 million. And while the outlook for the rest of the year was 'uncertain', by August 2009 Lord Bell was stating the company's portfolio of public sector clients had not been as affected by the economic downturn as the private sector and the company was doing very well due to its diversification.

PR is closely linked to lobbying and is one of the key routes to politicians. There's nothing underhanded about this as long as it's out in the open. Portland PR is proud of its government connections: 'Founded in 2001 by Tim Allan, a former adviser to Tony Blair and Director of Corporate Communications at BSkyB, Portland today has over 40 staff. Our team includes people from a wide variety of political backgrounds, former senior civil servants, journalists and professional communicators.'

We've seen the extent to which the main organs of the state are now saturated by PR, but no investigation of spin would be complete without a cameo from that most iconic of twenty-first-century state officials: the spin doctor.

The rise of the modern-day Iago

I imagine twenty years from now historians will look back and wonder how a small cadre of people lacking any productive skills were able to bamboozle whole industries and institutions into hiring them en masse and handing over to them key decision-making power. I'm talking about the rise of the public relations person, the spin doctor, the special adviser, the marketing guru. All these people create nothing but hot air. Occasionally they manage to add meaningful information to the world but their goal is not truth, rather the promotion of a politician or an institution. If that means censoring or fiddling facts in a way that is detrimental to the overall public good then so be it. These people may often be paid ultimately by the taxpayer, but their loyalty is to the politician or bureaucrat who hired them.

PR people have manoeuvred themselves right to the top of the political pole. Even senior managers have to get clearance from the press office to speak to the public, so that we're now in the bizarre situation whereby the people we elect can no longer communicate with us without the approval of unelected apparatchiks. One local council's communications guidance demonstrates exactly where the power now lies in public institutions: *Any manager or employee who receives a media inquiry should redirect it to the media team. It is not appropriate for officers to initiate contact with the media or respond to media enquiries independently without first consulting with the media team.*

John Brown, chairman of the Institute of Public Relations Scotland and elder brother of Gordon, explains why PRs are apparently so very important: 'The communicator is more and more the eyes and ears of the chief executive, giving him information about how he and his management team can deal with the issues they have to face. In that role, the communicator is now usually director level.'

How long can this continue? Politicians would do well to follow the advice of University of Westminster visiting professor of PR Trevor Morris: 'Quite often governments have used PR in lieu of hard policy. There have been lots of initiatives that turn out to be communications but not much else. Logically there are going to be big cuts in government budgets, so there is bound to be a cut in PR spend.'

The tough economic climate has prompted a few of the more enlightened officials to question the value of PR, but publicists are certainly not going hungry. Pam Calvert, managing director of Communications Management, told the industry magazine *PRWeek*: 'At this stage it is difficult to predict how cuts are going to impact on spending. However, we see this as an opportunity rather than a threat. Much of our public sector work is helping organisations diversify income sources [that's bilking the taxpayer of their hard-earned income in common parlance], so I would expect an even greater demand for external advisers who have this kind of expertise.'

When David Cameron pledged to cut the number of quangos to save money and boost accountability, the first thing some quangos did was – amazingly – look to hire a PR agency and waste even more money! There are some 790 non-elected quangos that spend nearly £43 billion a year, employing about 90,000 people. *PRWeek* reported that ConstructionSkills, the quango for the construction industry, 'is seeking an agency to work on stakeholder engagement. It is not known how this will affect its existing agency Fishburn Hedges.' Other PR agency sources told the magazine that Learn Direct and the Learning and Skills Council were also on the hunt for PR and marketing support. One agency managing director said: 'There have been a lot of briefs out from quangos recently. My sense is it's all about saying, "Look at us, we do a good job." It's about raising their profile and demonstrating their value for money because of concerns that there will be a cull.'

Yet again we see the PR scam in action. It's irrelevant whether you are providing value for money (which by hiring a PR firm clearly shows you're not); what's important is *appearing* to provide value for money. Associate director Graeme Buck of PR agency Camargue pronounces this typical emperor's-new-clothes assessment: 'Quangos are facing heightened levels of scrutiny and it makes sense to take professional advice on how to respond. Reputation management is as important for quangos as for any organisation.'

The sooner public institutions start respecting the expertise of their own people and the public's right to know, the sooner they'll win back public trust.

How spin works

Now we know what spin is, how can we spot it? Here are a few things to watch out for.

Pseudo-events

In his book *The Image* published in 1962, the American historian Daniel Boorstin first described the bizarre phenomenon whereby the reproduction or simulation of something becomes more real than its actual reality. It is hyperreal. He called such incidents pseudo-events as they had no real function except to promote something.

We could look at CCTV and any number of government crime-prevention initiatives as pseudo-events. There is no evidence that many of them work or indeed do anything at all except spend taxpayer money. But that is irrelevant in PR terms. What counts is that officials *appear* to be doing something. The problem is that because they are put in place for reactionary publicity purposes rather than in a thoughtful manner designed to actually address the problem, the problem remains and even more money is wasted.

We can see this technique in action in the way the government tried to fool the public about knife crime. After *Sunday Telegraph* reporter Ben Leach circumvented the Home Office's massive cadre of press officers to discover the truth about knife crime – that incidents were at least two-thirds higher than the previously announced official figures[1] – the response from a Home Office spokesman who refused to be named was: 'We have made it clear that tackling knife crime is a top priority and is not just about statistics . . . we want to make sure we get a full and accurate picture of what is happening to improve our understanding about crime on our streets.'

How did they do this? More cops on the streets? More efficient prosecution and sentencing of stabbers? No, they hired Kindred, a PR firm, to handle 'partnership marketing activity'. Although we don't know how much this campaign is costing as there's no press release about it, I would bet the knife campaign is chump change compared to the really huge campaigns such as the one spent promoting the disaster that is the National Programme for IT.

---

1. This was because the definition of knife crime had very little to do with whether a knife was actually involved.

Deference to authority

False optimism is the great enemy of democracy. Scepticism should be the watchword of all free societies: only believe what you can see with your own eyes, and take everything else with a pinch of salt until you can see for yourself if it works. The problem with public sector PR is that we are fundamentally less sceptical of, say, the Department of Health than we are of an oil company, simply because we expect the former – quite reasonably – to do what's in our best interest.

Appeals to fear

As one of the primary drivers of human behaviour, fear has long been recognised as a very effective way to control people, especially crowds. Because it's such a powerful weapon, appeals to fear must be scrutinised closely. Any time you hear a politician or official saying *We must do this, otherwise this terrible thing will happen* that's the moment to start demanding detailed data and facts. Usually, that's precisely the time you'll find these officials clam up or start spinning heavily because they have no facts to support their beliefs. Even when they do, mission creep will set in faster than you can say 'forty-two days', as the so-called 'war on terror' has shown. Fear is the weapon of choice for those politicians lacking real leadership ideas.

Claims of infallibility

We all make mistakes: you, me, bureaucrats, politicians, the police, judges. We are all human and no one, no institution, is infallible. Yet special advisers and spin doctors operate on a principle of never admitting fault. Can't we be treated by our leaders as grown-ups? Spin is costly for taxpayers because small problems aren't acknowledged, they are spun into successes or stifled until they reach a magnitude of catastrophic proportion. 'Success' in PR terms means positive coverage, but a stream of smiling councillors and puff pieces is not necessarily good for society. This myth of the infallible authority figure feeds into the general cynicism of the public. We all know politicians make mistakes and change their minds. We can see with our own eyes when something doesn't work. PR can effectively highlight one thing above another or put forward new angles of perception, but if something is fundamentally broken PR isn't going to fix it. If professionals could speak freely they might point out problems when they were small, or make suggestions for improvement. If the public had access to more information they could bring their own expertise and experience to the policymaking table and we'd all be better off.

The fact is that PR is always going to win, since even its own failings are immediately transformed into new market opportunities. If PR isn't improving an institution's reputation (and it never will in the long term) then what they sell is – more PR: Crisis Management or Reputation Management. Hence the appalling number of catastrophic, costly public service failures. The obvious solution to these disasters is to cut the PR and start devolving power down to individual staff members who know their business and allow these people the autonomy and freedom of expression to make suggestions and implement those suggestions. A public institution doesn't need to spend £1 million to improve its reputation. It just needs to deal forth-rightly and honestly with the public, to provide full facts behind decisions and policies, and – if a policy doesn't work – to try something else.

We have plenty of PR but we are starved of basic civic information. Here are my top five facts that every public body should provide to the people.

1. Line-item budgets – where the money's going, down to specific detail
2. Staff directories – the lobbyists have them, why not the electorate?
3. Organisation charts – who's in charge and how it all works
4. Notices of all meetings where decisions are taken that affect the public
5. Minutes of those meetings and all background briefings for policies and decisions

You can search all you want on any expensive government website but you won't find any public body offering all five of these basics. You'll be lucky to find a public service offering even one. You can chisel out some of this information using the FOI law but it's a thankless task. Bureaucrats will generally do all in their power to obstruct, delay or avoid answering your questions. Any secret society would be proud of what passes for communication in British public life.

It would be far cheaper and more efficient for the state to stop trying to micromanage and control public opinion. Let the facts speak for themselves. Let professionals speak out and let ordinary people into meetings where they can exert real power.

Instead we have no facts. Politicians push through policies for unknown reasons and thus the public are distrustful. As Nick Davies says in his excellent book *Flat Earth News*: 'The result is that all kinds of public debates which should be being settled on the basis of evidence and logic are instead being settled by the power of competing agencies to push their line.' It should come as no surprise that a recent survey by Local Government Communications showed the public's satisfaction with their council went down from 53 to 45 per cent as PR spending rocketed. In the end the only good PR is no PR. We need specifics, not sound bites. We want consistency and accuracy and a willingness from public officials to take responsibility and admit mistakes.

Whether it's CCTV, ID cards or turning a blind eye to girls forced into marriage, we have policies in place not because they are just, not because they are value for money, not even because they work – but because they allow a few powerful people to look good and, by looking good, to stay in power.

Thailand has a law against insulting the king. Turkey prosecuted award-winning writer Orhan Pamuk under Article 301 of the penal code for the offence of 'denigrating Turkey's national identity'. Brunei's constitution declares: 'His Majesty the Sultan can do no wrong in either his personal or any official capacity' and further admonishes that 'No person shall publish or reproduce in Brunei or elsewhere any part of proceedings that may have the effect of lowering or adversely affecting directly or indirectly the position, dignity, standing, honour, eminence or sovereignty of His Majesty the Sultan.'

We might laugh at such censorious laws from seemingly backward countries.

But just replace 'His Majesty the Sultan' with Bradford City Council or West Yorkshire Police and you get an idea of how deeply PR is infecting public institutions and destroying our democracy.

3

Bullshitting by Numbers:
Statistics, Targets and Lies

Facts can be fiction. Fiction can be fact.

How are you – poor member of the populace – to discern the difference between the two? Especially when the story-teller is spinning a tale woven from threads invisible to you? If it's the emperor's new clothes you're being sold, how can you tell a quality garment from one thrown together in a sweatshop? In this chapter my focus is not so much on the methodology of the statistician (after all, this is meant to be a readable book[1]) but on instances in public life where statistical manipulation has sold us counterfeit reality.

When former Home Office minister Vernon Coaker told MPs at a Commons question time that 'seventy police officers were hurt', for example, in a £5.9m police operation at Kingsnorth power station in Kent during August 2008, he

1. For a layman's guide to statistics and the ways they can be manipulated I recommend Ben Goldacre's book *Bad Science*, particularly the chapter 'Bad Stats'.

wasn't lying entirely but nor was he giving us the whole truth. Fortunately, a sceptical soul was dubious and used a freedom-of-information request to drill down into this quote for the actual raw data. It turned out that the injuries were nothing to do with the protestors as was insinuated – instead, the medical unit had dealt mostly with toothache, diarrhoea, cut fingers and 'possible bee stings'.

Or take the Labour government's move to liberalise pub opening hours in 2005. At the same time as this controversial bill was making its way through Parliament, the police stopped making arrests for drunk and disorderly behaviour and switched to using section 5 of the Public Order Act. Because the latter offence isn't specifically related to being drunk (it can be for any type of threatening or disorderly behaviour), it appeared as though alcohol-related crime had gone down when the reality was something quite different.[2] It was a similar story with Labour's efforts to cut hospital waiting times, a key policy promise back in 1997. Most of us would define 'waiting time' as the period between going to visit your GP and getting treated. The government,

2. Official police statistics are often a poor indicator of the nature and extent of public violence. In this instance when researchers at Cardiff University studied instead hospital admissions on alcohol-related injuries, they found a 47 per cent increase in admissions resulting from street fights in the five years since the licensing laws were changed. In 2002/3, before the introduction of the Licensing Act, there were 5,044 patients admitted after injuries from bar brawls; by 2008 this had risen to 7,432. This figure included minor injuries such as bites, kicks and scratches. The number of admissions for more serious types of violence, such as a sustained beating or an attack with a weapon, is far higher. The Cardiff University study estimated there were more than 350,000 such casualties in 2008.

though, measured instead the time between visiting a GP and seeing a consultant, just the first of two steps to getting treatment on the NHS. It's quite easy to manipulate this figure by simply directing consultants to see people more quickly. The patient isn't actually treated any earlier – the consultant might just provide a barrage of tests – so the waiting time from initial visit to treatment is no different at all. Here's where we begin to see why we should be sceptical when confronted by officials spouting statistics. Often the only thing official about them is that they advance an official's career.

Despite what we might believe about the decline of authority in public life, official figures still carry a lot of weight and it's precisely for this reason that politicians and others in authority enlist them to sell policy. If you want to hype success or hide failures, statistics are absolutely key. Statistics can make or break a policy and as a result make or break a political career. If you get elected on a platform of being tough on crime but the official figures come back showing crime is up, then you're probably not going to remain in office much longer. Depending on the stakes involved, the pressure on an official statistician to produce politically acceptable statistics can be enormous.

Government statistics make up four-fifths of all official statistics so it's cause for concern that British ministers get to see these far in advance of the general public. They have anything from twenty-four to forty-two hours to sift through and plan their PR 'line' or spin before publication. This pre-release period is one of the longest in the world. The United Nations recommends only a few hours to ensure the integrity of the statistics (i.e. that they haven't been interfered with politically). It is just one hour in France. The American president gets only thirty minutes.

It's easier to lie with statistics when the underlying data and methodology is kept hidden. For statistics to be trustworthy we should know precisely what is being measured (including all definitions of terms and recording rules), the methodology used for recording and measuring, and have access to all the raw data. Yet in the age of PR what you'll find is that getting hold of these three simple things is much harder than it need be. Bureaucracies are overly complicated, anonymity reigns, goalposts are shifted, definitions changed – so be it crime, health or education, officials are making it tough for us to separate fact from fiction.

Statisticians are forever lobbying for more independence in the UK. It was a Labour manifesto pledge to create an Office of National Statistics, under the pretence this would give statisticians the independence they needed to provide official figures free from political influence. The reality was that the head of the ONS reported to the Treasury and the Treasury controlled all the funding. (If your paymaster tells you to do something, what do you think the chances are of saying 'no'?) After a number of scandals, statisticians and the Royal Statistical Society successfully lobbied for greater independence and now the National Statistician, the head of the ONS, reports to a parliamentary committee rather than the Treasury minister. A new UK Statistics Authority was established in April 2008 to 'promote and safeguard the production and publication of official statistics that serve the public good' and its chairman is answerable to Parliament (although his staff are civil servants answerable to the government). There is a hope that this time the system *will* give statisticians the independence needed to regain public trust, which by 2009 had hit rock bottom,[3] but as we'll see in the knife-crime story below this independence is often sorely tested.

One of the first test cases of the new independent statistical authority was to re-examine road safety data, which for years had been massaged to give the impression that the roads had never been safer than in the ten years since Labour (and speed cameras) came into power.

Road safety – making the facts fit

Tot up the amount spent on speed cameras, road humps, road railings, etc., and you'll see that a whole industry has developed around certain ideas about what makes roads safer, alongside a whole generation of politicians whose policy reflects these beliefs. But are these beliefs based on anything other than fantasy? Do speed cameras actually cut accidents? Do humps in the road make us safer? If they don't, then it's money wasted and we need new road policies.

To any dubious journalist or sceptic who questioned whether roads were really safer in 2007/8 than ten years previous, the government would point to official statistics that showed a marked decline in the number and severity of accidents. This data was compiled by the Department for Transport based on traffic-accident forms completed by

3. Public trust in official figures was by this time the lowest in Europe, with only one in five people believing data was compiled without political interference, according to an ONS survey.

police in which they would indicate whether a person was killed, seriously injured, slightly injured or not injured. Based on these stats there is indeed a declining trend in the last decade. The problems arise when you look more closely into the data reported to the DfT by the police.

Road-accident statistics were first collected in the UK in 1909. The current system (known as STATS19 from the form police use to record accidents) was introduced in 1949 and reviewed in 1979. A STATS19 form is completed for all accidents reported to the police within thirty days of occurrence involving all road vehicles (including pedal cycles) and resulting in a personal injury. Accidents with pedestrians are included, as are accidents involving stationary vehicles. But *not* included are accidents where no one is injured (such as vehicle damage only) or where no road vehicle is involved (e.g. a pedestrian-only accident). Police forces undertake to record details of injury accidents they attend or which are reported to them but there is no statutory obligation on them to do this. This is the first indicator that these figures might not be all they're cracked up to be. What if a police force were to come under heavy political pressure to show a decrease in road injuries? With no obligation to publish raw police incident data or record injury accidents, it's not too much of a stretch to see how police can be incentivised into *not* reporting.

Then there's the form itself, which offers space for interpretation and thus manipulation. The police indicate on the form the level of injury: fatality, serious injury, likely injury or no injury. The government quotes only from the first two categories to measure road safety, so again there is an incentive to downgrade injuries from serious to 'likely'. And indeed that is what's been happening. A recent report by the National Audit Office noted 'there have been a number of studies of under-reporting, dating back to the 1970s, and from the limited data available it is estimated that there may be about twice as many casualties as are reported'. The chairman of the House of Commons Transport Committee said in July 2009 that the committee was 'extremely concerned' about the lack of reliability in road safety data, especially about serious injuries.

> Deaths on the roads declined by 18 per cent during the period that we were considering; serious injuries declined by twice as much. We questioned the accuracy of the recording of serious injuries on the road, and specifically that of the STATS19 system. We were disappointed that although the Government's response acknowledged that there might be a problem, they did not propose any steps that we thought would deal with it. I am thinking particularly of the discrepancies between some of the reporting of serious accidents and data received by hospitals. We want the Government to do more on that issue, as we are not satisfied that the information that we are getting is accurate.

Interestingly, evidence from the Department of Health on the number of people admitted to hospital after road accidents did *not* show a decline.

'This is a prime example of government following one set of data and putting pressure on the police to manipulate it while ignoring another set of data they can't manipulate,' says Simon Briscoe, author of *Britain in*

Numbers, a very readable and informative book on statistics.

Briscoe referred the road safety statistics to the newly created UK Statistics Authority as one of their first cases to test their independence. The authority acknowledged weaknesses in the DfT stats, noting, for example, that research conducted on behalf of the department showed that 'a significant proportion of non-fatal injury accidents are not reported to the police (in part because there is not always a legal duty to do so), and some which are reported are not recorded. Additionally there is evidence of a degree of underestimation of the severity of injuries in STATS19.' They asked the DfT for a more complete set of data but were told none existed. The DfT statisticians had tried to match up hospital records with police records but found numerous discrepancies due to police under-estimation of injury severity and changes to hospital admissions procedures.

The authority criticised the way the published statistics gave the public no indication of the extent of this missing data and injury downgrading, and complained that these stats were being touted by the government as a definitive list of road casualties: 'the under-reporting of road accident casualties is a significant and intractable problem. The Authority has concluded a) that the published statistics may not be sufficiently reliable to meet all user needs; and b) that DfT needs to explain and contextualise the limitations of the statistics more fully at the time of publication.' They suggested future publications be clearly labelled 'police recorded road casualty statistics' so it was clear they were not a definitive account of road casualties, and recommended publishing the statistician's name.

After all that, though, ministers still refer to the police figures as *the* definitive road casualty figures, claiming roads have never been safer. 'Ministers are incredibly reluctant to give up control of these numbers,' Briscoe says. 'What they don't want is some geeky statistician coming along telling them that actually things are getting worse since they introduced that policy.'

Which is precisely what needs to happen. We want problems fixed. We elect MPs and pay public officials to do this in our name and with our money. Success for us is when the problem is solved or alleviated, not when £12 million is spent on another advertising campaign. We can only judge whether a policy is a success from our own immediate experience and, more accurately, from the collected experiences of everyone else: so-called 'official statistics'. When those figures are manipulated we can no longer make an informed decision about what works and what doesn't.

In the case of road safety, we remain stuck with certain policies (speed cameras, street railings, bumps, etc.) because according to the official statistics the roads have never been safer. But now we know the figures are massively under-reported and the roads aren't as safe as we've been told, it seems sensible to question whether or not the current policies are actually working. They might, in fact, be a total waste of taxpayer money and also (in the case of speed cameras) an insidious stealth tax on motorists. Yet because these policies *appear* to work, we've carried on installing more speed cameras and following the same old policies. As long as things seem fine, why bother looking at other solutions? For example, there is a strong body of evidence that if the police cracked down on the drivers of unregistered cars and uninsured drivers, the number of accidents would fall dramatically. But this has not been a priority because as long as the government could point to the official figures that showed roads were safer there was no reason even to consider trying anything new.

Knife crime

Crime can kill a political career faster than anything. Most politicians at some point in their careers will make promises to be tough on crime. No one is ever going to say they're weak on crime but it would be nice to hear – just once! – a public debate infused with a bit of realism on the subject. Are we not adult enough to accept the fact that crime is a complex matter? That it is not always as simple as a children's fairy tale with goodies and baddies? Do we really believe it when a politician or policeman makes promises that he alone can save us from crime?

In order to have any kind of sensible public debate about crime we need detailed data about criminal incidents. What precisely happens where and when to whom by whom? This is the most basic information that any society needs to collect if it's serious about dealing with crime: we need facts, accurate information about what is happening in our neighbourhoods. Then we, the people who live in those neighbourhoods, can make informed decisions about the risks we take and help decide how finite resources should be spent tackling crime.

Instead, the general public have no access to timely,

detailed criminal incident data. We have to rely on officials to release the data to us in the format they choose, when they choose (often years after the fact) and the manner they choose (normally so vague that it is largely meaningless). People in power can't help fiddling with crime stats precisely because crime is such a politically contentious issue. The more they fiddle, the more they have to fiddle because the public lose faith in the validity of the stats. That's bad for democracy and bad for the public purse because it costs more money trying to convince people you're not a liar than if they trust you in the first place. We need crime data in its raw, unadulterated form, free from political interference. Until then we can be sold all sorts of stories about our safety – that we're safer than we actually are (thus we think the police and politicians are doing a better job than they actually are), or that we're more in danger than we actually are (so we're willing to hand over more of our individual freedom unnecessarily). I go into more detail about criminal justice in Chapter 7 but for now I want to focus solely on serious violent crime statistics, as these have been contentious for years but became a big story in 2008/9.

The government and police had been claiming that serious violent crime was falling, but what became apparent in 2008/9 was that these statistics were not presenting reality. In the same way road accidents were under-reported and injuries downgraded, the police were also under-reporting and downgrading the seriousness of violent crime.

By 2007/8 knife crime in particular had become such an issue that for the first time the Home Office asked police forces to provide data on serious knife offences. The only problem was the government defined 'serious knife offence' so narrowly it included only murder, attempted murder, robbery and grievous bodily harm, leaving out threats to kill and sexual offences where a knife was used. Under pressure from the police, the government extended the categories in 2008/9 (needless to say there were no press releases, PR stunts or public advertisements about the counting changes).

'The first I became aware of the change was when I was reading the "Crime in England and Wales" report,' said Ben Leach, the reporter for the *Sunday Telegraph* whom I mentioned in the previous chapter. 'I was reading the section about knife offences and buried in there I spotted that the definition of what was a serious knife crime had been expanded.'

Ben put in a freedom-of-information request for the first three months of the newly counted figures. 'They were saying they hadn't made a mistake but the whole point of them counting knife crime in the first place was to track trends and patterns. If you change the definition after just one year then you can't do any comparisons.'

The figures he received revealed that police forces in England and Wales were expected to record a total of 38,000 serious knife crimes in 2008 – more than a hundred a day. That figure was two-thirds higher than the previous year's total of 22,151 offences, published by the Home Office in July when it unveiled its first annual count of knife crimes.

After the official Home Office figures were released in October 2008, they showed an annual increase of one-fifth in violent attacks. The Home Office was forced to admit that police had failed to record serious violent crime accurately, with some forces possibly misreporting the figures for more than ten years. Yet even the new figures were not giving the full story, as some police forces were unable to provide up-to-date amended data. Ministers claimed at the time that two-thirds of the increase in serious assaults could be explained by corrections to previous downgrading (i.e. putting crimes in a lower category of offence). But it transpired that only one-third of serious knife attacks – which shot up nearly 30 per cent – were the result of such errors.

The government had continually been telling the public that crime was down. And overall it was, even according to the amended figures. For the three months to June 2008, the overall number of violent crimes was down by 7 per cent. But in two of the most serious violent crime categories it was a different story, for it was here that downgrading had been most serious. Attempted murders in England and Wales involving a knife between April and June 2008 rose by 28 per cent from the previous year, while assaults causing grievous bodily harm with intent rose by 29 per cent.

You can imagine, can't you, the dismay in Downing Street as these new knife crime stats came out just as another teenager was stabbed to death. As the headlines stacked up about the proliferation of knife crimes, the politicians did what came naturally: they fell back on the advice of their PRs and spin doctors to find ways of fooling the public. Instead of standing back, thinking about the problem, soliciting advice from experts, making all the data transparent so we might have an actual informed debate about the subject, the government acted in a typically reactionary and childish way. It looked for gimmicks, photo ops, celeb stumping, and stats they could spin. Gordon Brown launched the 'No to Knives' campaign with actress Brooke Kinsella –

whose brother Ben was murdered in a knife attack in 2008 – and Richard Taylor, the father of Damilola, stabbed to death in 2000. At this press-packed event he released 'official' statistics showing a 27 per cent drop in teenagers being taken to hospital with stabbing injuries at ten knife-crime hot spots identified by the government. The Home Office claimed serious knife crimes against young people were down 17 per cent between June and October 2008 in the ten areas targeted by the Tackling Knives Action Programme.

A great success!

Or was it? When some of the more sceptical reporters asked to see the raw data behind these headline figures they were refused access to the regional breakdown by the Home Office. Are alarm bells ringing yet? They should be. The next day the chairman of the UK Statistics Authority, Sir Michael Scholar, wrote to Number 10 about the government's 'premature, irregular and selective' use of the statistics. He'd learned that statisticians had been asked to provide figures not in their entirety but on a cherry-picking basis which breached the new code of conduct for official statistics that ministers had themselves approved to fend off accusations of spin.

'I discovered the impetus to do this came from within Number 10 Downing Street so I wrote to Jeremy Heywood [Permanent Secretary] in the PM's office to complain and also sent a copy of my letter to the Home Secretary,' Sir Michael told me.

It transpired that the 'official' figures released by the Home Office were nothing of the kind. They were provisional statistics of hospital admissions for knife or sharp-instrument wounding given to the Home Office by the NHS Information Centre not yet checked and not due for release until March of that year. When the professional statisticians working at the NHS Information Centre found out the figures would be used in a press release to sell the success of a government anti-stabbing campaign, they objected, and the National Statistician, Karen Dunnell, made representations to Sir Michael and 10 Downing Street before their publication. They were ignored. Sir Michael took the step (unusual in Britain) of publishing his letter to the PM's office on the Statistics Authority website, which led to, Sir Michael says with a mischievous chuckle, 'a great deal of interest and publicity'. Not long afterwards he received a written apology from Number 10 which he also posted on the site.

In February 2009 he was asked to give evidence about the controversy to the Public Administration Select Committee, who asked why he had written to Downing Street.

'I said I'd seen some emails which led to my conclusion that the PM's office was involved,' he told me, and reading back through the evidence the political influence is made clear.

> **Tony Wright** (*chair of the select committee*): My understanding is that the special adviser at the Department of Health was told by the NHS statisticians that this could not be published under the code. The special adviser went to the Number Ten special adviser to take advice on this.
> **Michael Scholar**: That's consistent with what I know.
> **Tony Wright**: Was it a proper decision for a special adviser to take?

Michael Scholar: The code of practice specifically bans political influence in the production of statistics. It is quite unequivocal under the code which was already in force.

The committee then asked Sir Michael if he would hand over the emails. Sir Michael had to think long and hard about this. Who was he responsible to? The government or Parliament (in the UK the public doesn't come into the equation)? If he'd been a civil servant his loyalty would have been to the government but because of the recent changes he was directly responsible to Parliament and so felt it was his duty to hand them his emails, which they duly published, creating a good deal more interest and publicity.

'The whole thing put me in a very difficult position,' he told me. 'On my authority sit three civil servants and their loyalty is to the Crown and prime minister. And it was they who gave me the information. I had a dilemma. Did I treat it as confidential as part of the government or as handed to me as a regulator and in which case I obeyed Parliament? After reflection I decided my primary responsibility was to Parliament and not ministers. I don't think I have any loyalty to ministers.'

When the official statistics (i.e. cleared by the official statisticians) were at last published in July 2009 they presented something quite different from those prematurely released by government. While the teenage homicide rate remained unchanged at 23, the number of adults over twenty who were fatally stabbed went up by 7 to 103. The 17 per cent drop quoted by government from hospital admissions figures was shown to be concentrated in London and Birmingham. In three of the ten targeted police forces (Greater Manchester, Nottinghamshire and Thames Valley) violent knife crime actually went up. The Metropolitan Police had three fewer knife-crime murders and the West Yorkshire force reduced teenage deaths from seven to zero during the campaign period. But Manchester saw the number of teenage murder victims of knife crime rise by four and the death toll on Merseyside rose by three. So overall, the £3 million spent in the ten targeted cities on PR, after-school police patrols and 250,000 stop-and-searches wasn't a great success.

Ironically, the response by ministers to these harsher figures wasn't to try something new but to draw out the failed campaign. Another £5 million was spent on the second phase of the tackling knives action programme: the number of targeted police forces was expanded to sixteen and widened to cover all forms of serious violence among 13- to 24-year-olds, including gang culture. Why admit you've made a mistake if you've money to burn pretending a failure is a success? It might be good for politicians but it's not good for the public.

Government interference isn't always so obvious and we must give credit to Sir Michael Scholar and the UK Statistics Authority for having the guts to go public about the heavy-handed political manipulation they faced. Maybe the statisticians have just decided enough is enough. After all, it wasn't as though the knife-crime press fiddle was unusual. It was actually the second time in a matter of months that the Home Office had been caught manipulating statistics for political ends. In August 2008, Professor David Hand, head of the Royal Statistical Society, had criticised serious bad practices during the release of immigration figures.

Immigration

Without getting all *Daily Mail* on you, I want to broach the contentious topic of immigration and why statistics are centre stage of this particular drama. I'm an immigrant to Britain while my parents were emigrants from Britain to America, so I've personally experienced both sides of migration. In America, immigration is a fact of life, so I find it odd that whenever anyone tries to discuss immigration in the UK they're immediately accused of racism. It's not racist to think about how immigration is going to impact on society. It's practical.

The only way to ensure public services are ready to absorb immigrants into local communities is to have some idea of how many there are. Amazingly, in the UK such data doesn't exist. This is not so much a case of spinning statistics but of having none whatsoever – the silent state rendered truly speechless.

New births and deaths must be registered by law but the same is not true for international migration – there is no systematic register that records all people entering or leaving the country, or where they settle. Instead, information on immigration and emigration is largely drawn from a sample survey conducted at ports called the International Passenger Survey (IPS) together with estimates done by the Office of National Statistics based on NHS patient registers. This doesn't seem particularly rigorous when you consider that international migration is, according to the UK Statistics Authority, the largest component of population change in the United Kingdom and has been since the late 1990s, when it exceeded the net effect of births and deaths.

While state involvement can often lead to unnecessary intrusion, one area where the opposite is happening is immigration. It wouldn't go amiss for British immigration officers to ask a question or two; maybe get non-citizens to fill out a form asking some questions about where they're from, where they're staying, where they're studying and for how long. Alarmingly, we have *no accurate measurement* of the net flow of people into and out of the country. This data is essential for reliable population estimates, which are in turn essential for government policy development, resource allocation and public services both nationally and locally. As it is, the UK government, the National Statistician and independent commentators have all concluded that official statistics of international and internal migration are currently inadequate, especially at regional and local authority levels. There is no exit data kept and improvements through the e-borders programme will not begin until 2010/11.

Immigration is a highly sensitive topic. But who is served by keeping the public ignorant about its extent? Some may argue that knowing the extent would encourage extremist groups such as the BNP and UKIP, but I would argue it's the state's refusal to be honest with its citizens that has done more to fuel prejudice than any disclosure of hard facts. Had proper data systems been in place we could have seen what the real numbers were instead of leaving us at the mercy of any sensationalist claim about asylum seekers taking over. Local authorities would have been able to plan so there would be an appropriate number of teachers available, for example, to teach English – ten years ago only 5 per cent of the student body were non-English-speaking whereas today that might be as high as 50–60 per cent in some communities. And we'd know how much additional social housing would be needed and whether this was something the tax base could handle.

It's not like officials were unaware of the problem. The lack of good data was identified from the beginning when immigration policy was liberalised, and various independent and government statistical committees, even the House of Commons Treasury Committee, have recommended that more and better migration data be collected. Yet it wasn't until 2009 that ministers finally acknowledged there was even a problem.

If we had decent data then we could have an honest debate about immigration policy. Instead we are left ignorant, and in the void where facts should be there is a space wide open to exploitation. The *Daily Mail* can claim we're overrun by immigrants and public services can't cope while the *Guardian* can claim precisely the opposite. These two contrary positions can only exist because at the heart of this debate, one where we should all be able to turn to empirical data, there isn't any. Patronising politicians argue we can't be trusted with the facts or we'll all vote BNP. I argue that's precisely the danger of *not* being honest with people. The first step in understanding something is to get the facts. We need good data about immigration and this data needs to be fed out to local councils who can then be in a better position to allocate funds. If councils are facing an undue burden housing immigrants then they should raise this publicly and tell us the extent of the problem. Then we can have an informed debate about whether it is the state's role to house people. We can't have that debate at the moment because we simply don't have the data.

Official statisticians are doing their best. They have lobbied hard for improvements in the data collected at airports and ports. They succeeded in getting into law the Statistics and Registration Service Act 2007 that allowed the ONS to gain access to student data from the Higher Education Statistics Agency to record the number of foreign students. Are you as surprised as me to discover that before this the ONS *didn't* have access to this? Here's a situation where there clearly is a legitimate need for data to be shared. And it wasn't.

What I hope you are beginning to see is the way ordinary citizens are constantly bearing the brunt of a lack of rigour, common sense and clear thinking by politicians and public servants. Instead of doing the necessary work of monitoring who enters the country, the government woefully fails in this task and then in a reactionary way doles out huge amounts of taxpayer cash to private IT firms to build massive surveillance systems on the British populace, the majority of whom are completely law-abiding.

Eyes wide open

Hiding from the truth does not make it go away. Ostrich-like behaviour by those in power succeeds only in prolonging a problem, usually making it worse. What we've seen is that a target-driven approach – with those targets set not by the people doing the actual work, nor by the public on the receiving end, but by bureaucrats in Whitehall – creates perverse incentives and even more perverse figures which, when exposed for what they are, damage not just public trust in government but society itself. National curriculum results for eleven-year-olds announced by press release claim that results were the 'best ever'; the reality is that 40 per cent of children failed to achieve the expected standard for their age in the combined results for reading, writing and mathematics. The government claimed success with record numbers of school-leavers getting A grades at A level; yet a report by Durham University revealed those same results would have got a C grade twenty years ago. The response from government to all these social issues is the same. It isn't to give us the facts so we can have a thoughtful, reasoned debate and come to the most sensible solution. It's instead what I call the PR-politician's four-point plan to losing public trust.

1. Resistance – first try to stop the public getting hold of pure, unadulterated data.
2. Interference – micromanage to the extent that other professionals cannot get on with their jobs. Set yardsticks that make you and your ideas look great and if that doesn't work, change them frequently.
3. Manipulation – once the figures come in, start spinning.
4. Smear – when all else fails, bully and attack any sceptics who fail to fall in line.

Crucially, even when we are able to obtain information that has not been 'filtered', we have to be ultra-vigilant. Matthew Davis is a veteran journalist who specialises in wheedling out information from big bureaucracy, going under the radar and making freedom-of-information requests to see what's really happening behind the hype.

Davis wanted to know, from the Department for Work and Pensions, the ailments for which people were claiming incapacity benefits. It seemed a straightforward query, but there was little point going to the DWP press office, which only releases anodyne quotes and its own positive news; so he put in a freedom-of-information request for the complete list of incapacity claimants broken down by individual illness. He was not asking for names (which was just as well because, as we'll see in Chapter 4, his chances of getting that would be less than winning the lottery). He received from the DWP a large Excel spreadsheet which listed all sorts of ailments in the far left column with the number of claimants to the right. He studied the data for some time. There didn't seem to be anything too shocking or surprising. In fact, the only surprise was the low number of claimants. He was happy to accept a good-news story if that was the case, but going on past experience he gave it one more look. It was then that he spotted something odd.

There were several types of illness listed that had zero claimants. 'I wondered, why list the category at all if there's nobody claiming on it?' Davis told me.

Fortunately he'd just been on an Excel spreadsheet course. He went into one of the cells listed as '0' and clicked on the 'format cells' button. The cell, he discovered, was formatted to show no decimal places and truncated to parts of 1,000 so, for example, 1,000 would show up on the table as '1', 2,000 would be '2' and anything less than '1' was therefore '0'. When Davis changed the cell formatting to show the exact number he found a wholly different set of data.

'Then you suddenly started to get loads of values appearing in these boxes. You were getting hundreds of people claiming for benefits where before it looked like there were none.'

Among his findings: nearly 2,000 people were claiming they were too fat to work and getting paid a total of £4.4 million in benefits. There were fifty people claiming benefits based on acne, sixty people with 'nail disorder' and ten leprosy. In total, Davis found 480 different types of ailments claimed by 2.7 million people who tapped the public purse for £7.5 billion.

He wrote up his story and *The Times* and *News of the World* ran it prominently under the headlines: 'TOO FAT TO WORK' and 'ZIT'S A JOKE'.

'I woke up that morning to Radio 4's *Today* programme and there was Peter Hain [minister at the time] saying "This story is absolute rubbish" and he dismissed it as a total fiction. Throughout the day his comment was put forward as a counterweight to the facts which I'd uncovered and no one – not one journalist – challenged him that these were *his own department's figures*.'

Some eighteen months after Davis filed this request, he put in another seeking updated figures. This time, the DWP (on the advice of their press office no doubt) claimed they didn't keep the statistics in the same format and stated that if he wanted them it would mean creating an entirely new database which would cost too much so the request was rejected. Davis is sceptical and has appealed, yet it's worth stressing that this is not an isolated occurrence. When Davis inquired about the number of drug-and alcohol-addicted mothers and babies treated by the NHS – a legitimate public-interest story as it costs a lot of money to treat drug-and alcohol-addicted mothers and babies, and resources are finite in the NHS – he was told the figures had miraculously disappeared from one year to the next. Or to put it into bureaucratese: 'The information is not available in the format requested for 2007/8. The overall figure (not broken down by PCT) is available via a tailor-made report, from the HES Online website (www.hesonline.nhs.uk), in the form of a tabulation or an extract of the raw data.'

For this there would be a substantial charge. Not only that but he would have to sign a twelve-page document outlining what he planned to do with the data, who he would share it with and his motivation for asking for it in the first place. Can we just remember: this is public data which the public has paid for and which the public have an interest in knowing. No one should have to justify to a public servant why they want public data. It belongs to us.

Getting priced out of the marketplace of public information isn't unusual. There are hundreds of incidents where the only people benefiting from public data are the richest and most powerful. But before we go into that we need first to steel ourselves and deal with a most uncharismatic and unpopular creature – the Bureaucrat.

4

The Corridors of Power

I don't know how it happened. It wasn't intentional, believe me. I can think of more thrilling things to become in life than an expert on British bureaucracy. My passion is investigative journalism, but as I was trained to play by the rules and seek facts through legitimate means it wasn't long before I found myself chin-deep in the petty diktats and overall unhelpfulness of one of the world's oldest bureaucracies.

Bureaucracy is the business of controlling other humans, making them do what you want them to do. That may be acceptable if what you are asking them to do is reasonable, rational and for the common good, but more likely what bureaucrats ask is *un*reasonable, *non*sensical and *counter*-productive to the public good. This is because the primary business of a bureaucrat, left unchecked, is creating more bureaucracy to further his or her own prestige and power. The result is that rules are in place serving no function but to keep bureaucrats in work and to expand their bureaucratic fiefdom. Before you know it you can't even hold a village fete without filling out more than fifteen different forms from various arms of the government.

There's a painting by Salvador Dalí that well illustrates the qualities of officialdom. It's called *The Average Bureaucrat* and it depicts a man in a landscape barren except for a few rocks. His body is smooth, his head an oval, featureless apart from two openings: one where the eyes would be and another for a mouth. There are no ears. That's the bureaucrat: always telling us what to do, never listening. It seems entirely fitting that the man who came to define surrealism picked a bureaucrat for his subject. Bureaucracy *is* surreal, as Dalí, whose own father was part of the ignoble profession, well knew.

Here's a little pin-up guide for what makes a good and bad bureaucracy. The day I see this in any public body I'll know my work is done.

Good Bureaucracy	Bad Bureaucracy
All officials named	Anonymity
Devolved power and responsibility given over to professionals and front-line staff	Centralised, top-down hierarchy. Professionals stripped of power
No new bureaucracies without a clear statement of costs and a majority legislative vote of approval	New bureaucracies created at whim by executive with no public disclosure of costs
Detailed (e.g. line-item) and transparent budgets	Budgets hidden or overly vague
Involvement in individuals' lives confined to an absolute minimum	Involvement in every aspect of individuals' lives

Going through this list it should be pretty clear into which camp British bureaucracy falls. It ticks every box on the right and none on the left. I am constantly amazed at the way officials can magic into existence an entirely new quango, for example, or department – such as the 'Independent' Parliamentary Standards Authority, which we'll encounter again in Chapter 8 – without giving a detailed public account of the costs involved. Existing departments have budgets broken down only by vaguely defined subject areas that obscure from the public the precise amounts spent.[1]

What I hope to do in this chapter, then, is lift the grey rock of officialdom and have a good look at what's underneath, examining the freakish creatures that scrabble out, scared of the sunlight of public scrutiny. Far from merely complaining about bureaucracy, I want to propose a solution. It's not the solution put forward by the bureaucrats themselves – namely creating *more* bureaucracy to cut bureaucracy (witness the ludicrously titled Bureaucracy Reduction Group, comprised entirely of bureaucrats). No, I argue that two things must be done if we're serious about slashing bureaucracy and making officialdom work for citizens.

1.   There must be a political move to end bureaucrats' proprietorial hold over official information: public

1. While some councils are starting to provide the taxpayer with more detail about how their money is spent a simple, national fix would be to open up the government's COINS database, which is used by the Treasury and other departments to monitor and control spending. If the Treasury can't make it accessible I know plenty of IT developers in the non-profit sector who would be only too happy to help, some of whom are mentioned in the next chapter.

information must be owned by the people and freely available to the public who paid for it and in whose name it is collected (more on this in Chapter 5).

2. Bureaucrats must be named and held individually accountable for what they do. Ending anonymity is the most critical reform that must happen if bureaucracies are to work *for* people and not against them.

If there's one thing I've learned from my many wranglings with various officials it is that they love anonymity. To be a known individual breaks all the rules of the diktatery (dictatorship by diktat): it shatters the facade of unbreachable power which is how these institutions preserve the illusion of godlike authority, and allows officials to exercise power without being accountable for their decisions and/or actions. Remember these people are public servants and they are paid to serve you and me. We have every right to know who they are. There's nothing private about what a public official does in his official capacity. These people need to get over their paranoia and realise their job is serving the public.

Breaching the faceless wall of bureaucracy

The key to battling big bureaucracy is simple: find out where the power lies. Specifically, by name. Who made the decision? Who sent the email? Who made the allegation? Passed the policy? Or stood by passively while the policy was passed?

Don't be content with getting the name of the top person in charge – you want the names of *all* people involved. If an official is exercising power that affects the public then he should be accountable for what he's doing or has done. That's only right and fair.

It's only by breaking down bureaucracy into identifiable individuals that you have any chance of success. Bureaucrats know this and that's why they do all in their power to remain anonymous. Why do you think the police take off their numbered badges when they're going to get medieval on some innocent protestor? It's not because they're proud of what they're about to do, it's because they want deniability: to exercise power without being held individually accountable.

A good example of the power of naming comes from the film *Schindler's List*, in which German businessman Oskar Schindler saves the lives of nearly a thousand Jewish refugees during the Second World War by employing them in his factories. When he encounters the unthinking obstruction of officials he takes out a notebook and asks the officials' names. They're about to be identified! You can see the worry in their eyes as they're faced with a dilemma: either they refuse and look cowardly, as though they're ashamed of what they're doing, or they give their names and become individually responsible for their actions. The official then has to do something very rare – he must think about what he is doing. Is it sensible? Ethical? What the dear leader actually wanted? Once you put a face and name to an official you strip them of the power of anonymity. To see what a difference this makes I recommend the following experiment.

How to make a helpful bureaucrat
- Take one immovable, obstructive, unthinking bureaucrat.
- Step 1: attempt to talk sense to and/or reason with this person. (Note the lack of response – remember he has no ears!)
- Step 2: ask for the bureaucrat's name and the name of his or her manager. (Note the sudden change of behaviour, which may follow the familiar pattern of defensiveness > aggression > resignation > grudging helpfulness.)

Staff directories vs ID cards

Here's another little experiment. I want you to think about something which most of us have probably accepted without question: the introduction of national ID cards and, more importantly, the database that underlies them. This will include fifty items of our personal information, including *all* our addresses, contact details, education, etc. Now think about government staff directories. These are lists of contact details for public servants who are paid by us. They include names and work contact details (we're not talking home telephone numbers or personal email accounts, just official work contact info). The ID database contains very intrusive information about private citizens going about their private business and yet the government feels entitled to spend billions of pounds of our money to create this system. Contrast that with the way these same government officials refuse to allow the public access to staff directories in which non-intrusive contact details are collected.

If you're opposed to ID cards, go and work for the Identity and Passport Service (a new bureaucracy created by the Home Office). With the usual irony, this public body refused my freedom-of-information request for the names of staff working on the ID card project in the very same week that the project was approved! It was only by using other means that I discovered 186 staff were working on the ID project: 54 civil servants, 98 consultants and 34 interim staff.

It's one rule for them and another for us.

We need transparency of the state and privacy for the private citizen but instead what we have today is the exact opposite. There should be nothing secret about the identity of those working in your local council, or indeed the names of those in the Ministry of Defence who broker arms contracts. But obtaining this very basic information about public officials is almost impossible in Britain. Of course, there are many illicit means of getting hold of a staff directory. I have quite a few in my possession. But any member of the public ought to know who is working on their behalf. You shouldn't have to wine and dine an arms dealer to get hold of the Ministry of Defence staff directory.

Anonymity and the arms trade

Rob Evans wanted the staff directory of the Defence Export Services Organisation (DESO), a hived-off part of the Ministry of Defence, which spends taxpayer money helping UK arms companies (predominantly BAE Systems) win contracts for the export of armaments several reasons.

'We were hearing a lot of allegations about co within DESO in relation to the arms industry,' Rob told h 'The problem was you had to find out if the employee alleged to be accepting bribes from an arms company actually worked for DESO. There was no way to tell. In the absence of a staff directory we had to resort to, well, subterfuge. It was done in the public interest but in my view that's wrong. Why should we have had to resort to subterfuge? All public officials should be named.'

The Data Protection Act is often used in the most ludicrous ways: reporters' bylines blacked out and ministers' names censored. If you're a public official then suddenly your privacy rights are sacrosanct. DESO and the Ministry of Defence were none too keen to provide Rob with a copy of the directory, so from his desk at *Guardian* newspapers he filed a freedom-of-information request in January 2005. The directory lists staff names, job titles, work addresses, work telephone numbers and email addresses. In February he received a 'redacted' or, in plain English, censored version. And when I say censored I mean heavily. You've likely seen the 'redacted' MPs' expenses, but imagine something even more gratuitous. What Rob received was a staff directory with *all* the names of staff together with *all* their contact details removed. Even the main switchboard number was blacked out! Only titles remained and for staff based in Saudi Arabia even these were excised. As a staff directory it was pretty much useless, particularly if your purpose was to track staff movement through the revolving door that exists between DESO and the arms industry and vice versa.

...e the usual – national

... Act (e.g. privacy) – but

... exemptions such as disclo-

... e effective conduct of public

... would 'endanger the physical or

... als. I doubt any of us would have

... h excuses to the government if we

... eillance.

... the Information Commissioner and won his case ... MoD fought on, spending £75,000 of public money to sto the public finding out who worked for them (an irony not at all unusual). The case went to the Information Tribunal where Rob argued that the 'revolving door' that existed between government and the arms industry had created a dangerous conflict of interest, whereby the government was working in the interests not of the public but of private arms companies. And it wasn't just senior officials getting schmoozed. David Leigh, the *Guardian*'s investigations editor, cited the directory as necessary in a case involving John Porter, a £28,000-a-year DESO official who, evidence showed, had taken gifts including free holidays from arms firm executives. He retired before any action was taken. The newspaper knew of the story at an early stage but was reluctant to publish without proper verification, which the directory would have provided.

Censoring the names wasn't only wrong but ridiculous, as many were already in the public domain in military lists and the Civil Service Year Book. In addition, Rob discovered the directory wasn't exactly top secret. It was given to a few friendly journalists and employees of a news agency who covered the defence industry. Most shocking of all, the directory was handed out at arms fairs to manufacturers and consultants in the arms trade.

John Millen, then director of Export Services Policy in DESO, said at the tribunal hearing: 'A copy was provided if the request came from a member of the UK Defence Industry or if the requester concerned had an accepted reason for doing business with DESO.' Mr Millen then confirmed that in 2004, about 2,000 copies of the directory were sent to 'named individuals at external addresses, including other government departments'.

Just to hammer home the point that DESO was working for the arms industry and not the public, a reminder was printed on the cover of new directories stating it was for government and industry use only. Sadly this attitude remains unchanged across most public bodies.

It was alleged by the MoD that official business would be hindered if the public were allowed to know who was working for them and how to contact them directly. Think about that for a minute: a public body operating on the principle of cordoning itself away from the public; the public seen as a nuisance rather than the sole reason they have a job. What it smacks of is that paranoid pomposity so typical of public officials, and reveals two main fallacies they commonly hold about the public at large: a) that the average citizen is civically active in a way that all evidence shows they are not (e.g. we are not all busting a gut to phone up the Secretary of Paperclips), and b) that the average citizen is a criminal (in fact, most people are perfectly polite and reasonable if treated with respect and listened to).

The usual made-up disaster-movie scenarios were put forward by the MoD: that we'd all rush out to get a copy of the directory and then get busy stuffing envelopes full of anthrax to DESO staffers. Are the British people uniquely dangerous? I don't think so. (Though judging by the numerous signs on display in every British institution, we're some of the most violent people on earth.) There's never any evidence put forward for these scare stories because that's exactly what they are – tall tales told to suit the bureaucrats' love of exercising power unaccountably.

The Information Tribunal ordered the directory to be published, though it did allow anonymity for junior staff, which was problematic. However, by then (20 July 2007) Rob Evans was already in possession of a leaked staff directory.[2] From their illicit 2005 copy, the *Guardian* reporters discovered some interesting facts: more than 450 civil servants worked in DESO with 161 civil servants working specifically for the 'Saudi armed forces project' across Britain and the Middle East. All told, 'around 40 per cent' of staff, a minister admitted, was dedicated to selling to one regime: Saudi Arabia. Also interesting when you consider that at the time DESO was headed by former BAE executive Alan Garwood, who was interviewed by the Serious Fraud Office over long-running government-authorised £1billion payments to Prince Bandar of Saudi Arabia. Both BAE and Prince Bandar said the payments were legitimate but when Tony Blair was prime minister he halted the SFO inquiry, again citing 'national security'. The US Department of Justice then began its own investigation.

That so many UK civil servants, paid for by us, are promoting arms to an autocratic regime in an unstable area

2. As we'll see again, sadly in the UK trying to get information legitimately is always the least effective method.

is clearly a subject worthy of public debate. Without the directory this information was hidden and no debate could take place.

The average bureaucrat

In the UK, the best way of preserving your privacy is to become a public official. Even local council staff are loath to tell us who they are and how we can contact them. While working on an article back in 2005 I got this gem of a quote from Peter Mead, then the corporate information officer at the London Borough of Barking and Dagenham. He refused to let the public have access to the council staff directory. 'Publishing our directory would cause untold confusion,' he said. 'We have put a lot of money into our call centre, so we don't want members of the public calling up employees directly.'

This made me laugh. I grew up in Seattle where you can go online right now and find the name, direct telephone number and email of public employees (http://www.seattle.gov/directory). Not only can residents find out who is in charge of various departments, they can drill down to see who is collecting their rubbish, who sweeps the street, who is enforcing dog-control ordinances or even filling potholes.

'We call that accountability,' Dewey Potter told me. She was working in Seattle's parks and recreation department at the time. 'It would be a disservice to the public not to give out those names. We're public employees. We work for the public and the public are our boss. They have a right to know who we are and what we do.'

Tell that to the civil servants who like to quote the so-called Osmotherley rules whereby civil servants are accountable only to ministers and not directly to Parliament and certainly not (eee gads!) to the public. And don't get me started on the archaic tradition of ministerial 'collective responsibility', which is merely a euphemism for collective *ir*responsibility.

The UK has a long tradition of secrecy in this area going back at least seven hundred years. Cabinet secrecy arises from the Privy Councillor's Oath, which provides the only constitutional definition of a government minister. This oath states that the minister will 'keep secret all matters committed and revealed unto you, or that be treated of secretly in Council'. Secrecy was put into a legal framework with the passage of the Official Secrets Act in 1911. Although there were few prosecutions under the Act, its main purpose was to intimidate public servants and discourage them from speaking directly to the public, even if to do so was vitally in the public interest.

In railing against anonymity, I'm actually doing bureaucrats a favour. They won't thank me for it, I'm sure. But this culture of silence and buck-passing isn't doing state workers any favours. It keeps the worst people in the most lucrative, high-end jobs while the best go unrewarded, often punished for speaking out. It allows bad practices and in-efficiencies to continue while good ideas get shelved and ignored. It robs people of their individuality and independence since staff members are not allowed to 'own' their work, which is crucial if they're to take any pride in it. Secrecy's main advantage is that it allows people to express opinions and exercise power without being individually accountable. There may be some instances – such as initial brainstorming – where that is warranted, but an entire system of government based on a default position of secrecy is nothing less than totalitarian. If the opinion or decision is a good one then it should be able to withstand public scrutiny. If it cannot, then one must be sceptical that it was a wise decision. Most likely it was based not on reason but unreasoned prejudice, untested beliefs or outright stupidity.

The faceless wall of anonymity doesn't just disengage and alienate citizens from institutions, it destroys the morale and professional pride of staff working in these institutions. Failure is rewarded while merit ignored. That's to be expected in a system based on patronage rather than performance, where secrecy and anonymity are the twin totems used to protect the incompetent, and transparency is seen as dangerous because it highlights the poor quality of those in positions of power.

Bureaucracies are interest groups like any other. Arms traders, pharmaceutical companies, environmental groups, unions: all are looking to promote their particular point of view. What is a bureaucracy promoting? Surely they work for us and their business is to serve the people? That is true only if officials account *directly* to us and the information they hold in their possession is freely available. If not, then very quickly officials come to work for themselves, their modus operandi the same as that of all other organisms: to maintain and expand their power. Success, in bureaucratic terms, is measured by size. They want bigger budgets, more staff and more perks.

Anonymysing spokespeople

There is one group who, by the very definition of their role, have absolutely no reason to be anonymous. These

are official spokespeople. Yet one of the more dubious practices of the British press is the way reporters collude with
officials by granting them anonymity. Sources should be
granted anonymity only in very limited circumstances where
naming may cause specific harm (such as a whistle-blower
who could lose his job). There is no reason a Home Office
spokesman, for example, should be granted anonymity, yet
I've had many arguments with these people who insist on
it as their 'right'. Meanwhile, they demand to know all about
me – my name, my publication, what my 'angle' is, etc. I
usually do get their names from email correspondence and
print them in the newspaper. So far the sky has not fallen
and I've not been locked up for giving a name to the usually
nameless mouthpieces.

Although they will tell you it's because they are not
speaking as an individual but in the place of someone else
or an institution, the real reason spokespeople don't want
to be named is no different from that of the policeman
who removes his badge before assaulting a protestor: deniability. Official spokespeople are powerful because they
speak for the powerful; anonymity means they can exercise that power without being held individually accountable
for it. They make pronouncements that impact the public
directly and yet the public have no idea who has said what.
It's not good enough to say they are speaking for someone
else.

We all know about Alastair Campbell, the king of spin,
but did you know that for most of his career as Tony Blair's
spokesman he was anonymised by the press? The public
simply had no idea he was the one saying the things that
were said. Only after he was unmasked – a face and name

put to the 'official spokesman' – did he become individually accountable for what he said. And perhaps not surprisingly it was shortly afterwards that he resigned.

When a 'spokesman' makes an accusation or spreads a smear, what recourse is there for the target? Anonymising spokespeople suits some journalists because if every source is simply a 'spokesman' or 'official' then it's easy to make up any old quote to suit your story. As a reader you should be sceptical of such quotes. The source of news (*who* said it) is just as important as what is said. It's much trickier to put imagined words into a named individual's mouth (and when that does happen there are sanctions that person can take against the reporter or source).

Reporters in the US are told always to fight against officials' attempts to be anonymous. I believe this is a fundamental role of the journalist: to push officials to stand behind what they say. If they don't agree, then don't print it or give it airtime. It really is that simple. If journalists stuck together on just this one point, they could overnight force a change in the culture of Parliament, the Civil Service and many public services.

Why naming matters: the case of the Speaker's speaker

For reporters covering Parliament, December is a difficult month. The House of Commons is in recess and MPs are away for five weeks. To fill the gap, Simon Walters of the *Mail on Sunday* put in a freedom-of-information request for the details of the taxi claims made by the Speaker's wife. The reply came (perhaps not coincidentally) over the

Christmas break when Walters was away on holiday. Just to ensure he didn't get the scoop he clearly wanted, the Commons posted the answer on the Web, which is where another reporter, Sam Coates of *The Times*, found it. The reply stated that the wife of Speaker Michael Martin had claimed £4,280.20 since May 2004 on 156 taxi journeys, mainly for shopping trips.

'I called the Speaker's office to ask about these claims,' Sam Coates told me. 'It was difficult because around Christmas the House isn't sitting. But I do remember I was given this number for a guy called Mike Granatt who didn't even work at the House of Commons. I seem to recall I woke him up and he was in some foreign country and I remember thinking "Isn't it ridiculous that I have to call some guy halfway round the world to find out what the Speaker is doing just a few yards away from me?"'

Mike Granatt is an experienced communications consultant. He is a partner at the Luther Pendragon PR agency, and former director of the Government Information Service. In 2007/8 he was working as media adviser to the House of Commons Commission, the management committee chaired by Michael Martin (more on Martin in Chapter 8). The Speaker was at that time under heavy criticism both for his handling of the MPs' expenses scandal but also his own very liberal expense claims. Plus he was using public money to employ a private PR firm.

Sam asked Mike Granatt about Mary Martin's taxi bill as he'd found that even some MPs were critical of the amounts claimed, which were more generous than their own allowed taxi claims.

'He came back saying the reason was that she was shopping for official functions. I thought this was absolutely ludicrous,' Sam said. 'The idea that Mary Martin was coming back from Waitrose with bags of food for official functions rather than hiring a caterer – well, it didn't pass the most basic journalistic smell test. I asked him: "Are you sure?" He said: "Yes. That's the explanation." He got quite defensive when I pressed him further. I actually thought he was trying to pull the wool over my eyes. I felt he wasn't trying hard enough to get to the bottom of things so I did something I don't normally do, which is I named him.

'It was a way of making him take personal responsibility for his quote because I didn't believe it and I thought he hadn't done enough to get to the bottom of what was actually going on.'

Most newspapers repeating Sam's story followed the usual convention and gave the Speaker's justification anonymously:

A spokesman for Mr Martin said: 'She goes shopping for food for entertaining official visitors.'

A Commons spokesman said: 'The burden on a Speaker's family can be great at times.'

However, Sam's report in *The Times* stated:

Mike Granatt, a spokesman for Mr Martin, justified Mrs Martin's claim. 'She goes shopping for food and so on for entertaining official visitors. The Speaker entertains periodically. There is a budget that is held for the Speaker's office and the money comes from that,' he said. He confirmed that Mrs Martin was not employed by her husband in any capacity.

Granatt said the Speaker was justified in putting through his wife's claims as the trips were 'entirely in connection with household expenditure that supports the Speaker's duties', adding that Mrs Martin needed to take taxis to shop for food for official functions. To underline the official nature of the shopping trips, he said Mary Martin had always been accompanied by an 'administrative official'.

Simon Walters came back from holiday and, suspicious of the line about the 'administrative official', set about to uncover who that person was. A few months later, he discovered the 'official' was none other than Mrs Martin's housekeeper and friend, Gloria Hawkes, and, not surprisingly, it was questionable whether the shopping was for any official purpose. Some of it was clearly for the couple's personal consumption – once a month Mrs Martin would do her shopping at a large supermarket and keep a taxi on a 'wait and return' basis, because (she later told a parliamentary investigator), they were 'not easy to hail'.

'We asked the Speaker's office about Mrs Speaker's shopping trips with Gloria Hawkes and they denied it,' Simon Walters told me, 'saying Mrs Speaker took an unnamed official to help get items for official receptions. It was a blatant fib. When Mike Granatt found out that it *was* Mrs Hawkes and the trips were personal, not official, he resigned. His statement on 23 February included a personal apology to me (a rare experience).'

The new reality directly contradicted the previous statement and because Mike Granatt was individually linked to what he'd told Sam Coates back in December he did *not* have deniability. And so:

> I have stepped down from my post for ethical reasons, because I misled a journalist unwittingly. It is core to the ethical code by which I and my company operate that I tell the truth, and that I am given the truth to tell. However, I learned on Friday that I had been led to mislead journalists over material facts in a story concerning the Speaker's household and the use of taxis. I have expressed my regrets to the journalist who brought this to my attention, and I offer them to anyone else who was similarly misled.

Asked by MPs on the Public Administration Committee to say who had misled him, Mr Granatt said he was 'not prepared to go into details of names or places . . . It wasn't the Speaker and it wasn't, as it was put to me, Mrs Martin.'

If Sam Coates hadn't taken the unusual decision of breaking the convention in the British press of naming the Speaker's speaker, would he have felt the same pressure to resign?

It begs the question – why are journalists colluding with officials by granting them anonymity and thus deniability? Most of the reporters covering Parliament don't agree with my stance on naming. I find this depressing. If *they* don't fight for the public's right to know, who else will?

'In practice the reason we don't do it is that frankly people won't talk to you again if you name them,' Sam Coates said. 'It would take a decision at editor level that we would do it en masse. If I was to do it unilaterally then the effect would be a huge amount of anger and a lot of people not talking to me unless I gave a guarantee that I wouldn't do it again.'

This should make it clear just how important anonymity is to the bureaucrat. If it didn't matter they wouldn't fight so hard to preserve it. The reason they do is because very often statements given by a 'spokesman' don't stand up to the slightest public scrutiny. It doesn't happen every day but too often anonymous quotes turn out to be biased, misleading or just plain lies.

To smear in secrecy: the case of Guido Fawkes and Damian McBride

The year 2007 was meant to see the end of spin, yet you only had to read the newspapers to see how the 'insider', 'senior source' and 'friend of the prime minister' was using anonymity to spread rumours, innuendo and accusations without ever having to be accountable for what was said. Here are some of the notable attack quotes and demolition jobs from that time (emphasis added):

> **10 September 2006** 'Gordon Brown's *allies* last night suggested that drink may have played a part in Charles Clarke's extraordinary attack on the Chancellor when he accused him of being a deluded control freak with psychological problems. *Friends of* Mr Brown have seized on the former Home Secretary's latest interview, in which he delivered a devastating assessment of the Labour leadership favourite, while clutching "a glass of red wine in his hand".'

2 April 2006 'At one stage this weekend, *sources close to* Mr Brown referred to their counterparts in Mr Blair's camp as madmen.'

21 March 2007 '*Friends* poured scorn on Lord Turnbull [the former Permanent Secretary who accused Brown of being like Stalin] as an embittered ex-official who was never highly rated and was kept out of the Chancellor's inner circle.'

No one can match for sheer nastiness the mud-slingers in the Downing Street bunker. It's only in a culture of anonymous sourcing that such smear tactics survive. So not surprisingly it took someone *outside* the parliamentary lobby to expose the chief smearer. Most lobby journalists knew all about Damian McBride but – crucially – the public did not because of the press convention of granting officials anonymity.

Damian McBride had been a member of the prime minister's inner circle for nearly a decade. He was a career civil servant and played a lead role in the Treasury's response to the fuel protests in 2000. He was spotted by Gordon Brown and became head of communications at the Treasury in 2003 and Brown's special adviser in 2005. Reporters knew him as a fearsome spin doctor who ruthlessly promoted Brown. Those journalists who dared go against him received aggressive text messages about their stories.

Then in early 2009 the political blogger Guido Fawkes (aka Paul Staines) broke convention and named McBride on Andrew Neil's *Daily Politics* show as the source of various smears. Things heated up even more when Staines came into possession of a series of emails sent by McBride to another Labour spin doctor, Derek Draper, in which they proposed a campaign of unfounded personal attacks against senior Conservatives, many of a sexual nature, that would help to 'destabilise' the opposition in the run-up to the general election. Charlie Whelan, Mr Brown's former spin doctor, was also copied in.

In the emails, McBride detailed four possible stories to ensure that a new Labour website would start off with a bang. He described the first story, about a gay Tory MP promoting his companion's business interests in the Commons, as a 'solid investigative story', suggesting that it 'may be a good one to use early'. The other three, he admitted, were 'gossipy and mainly intended to destabilise the Tories'. The mooted stories – all vehemently denied – were based on rumours about the personal lives of George Osborne, David Cameron and Nadine Dorries.

It's important to remember, in light of what happened next, that if the emails hadn't been leaked to Paul Staines then the smears would likely have gone into the public domain without any name attached. Official anonymity = total deniability.

No one should be surprised at the depths to which dirty politics can sink when people don't have to stand behind what they say. Fortunately, however, these two spin doctors *did* have to stand behind what they said because Staines gave the emails he'd obtained to the *Sunday Times* and *News of the World*. Initially, the prime minister's office tried to pass off the emails as juvenile banter, but with the smears attributed to Damian McBride *by name* his position was clearly untenable.

'This is far beyond the usual rough and tumble of politics,' Staines said, 'these are sexual smears, some so obscene you could not print them. Damian McBride is the prime minister's special adviser on press and politics, not some kind of juvenile in the background.'

McBride resigned soon after publication. Are these not lessons enough that all official spokespeople should be named?

A fatal lack of accountability

There are many other examples where the convention on official anonymity has dire consequences. After the 2002 train crash in Potters Bar which killed six people and injured many others, the first reports placed blame on engineering company Jarvis for shoddy maintenance. Then crisis-management PR flunkeys waded in, putting it about through unattributed briefings, where they were quoted only as a 'senior rail source', that the crash was more likely a result of vandalism. It wasn't until three years and an official inquiry later that the truth came out: vandalism was 'highly unlikely' and the probable cause was poor maintenance by Jarvis.

In June 2006, Scotland Yard raided a house in Forest Gate, east London, and shot an unarmed man. Senior officers gave unattributed statements to the press, saying the house was used for chemical terrorism (despite no evidence that this was true). They also smeared the residents, saying they had a suspiciously large amount of cash (they were Muslim and didn't use banks), and that one had downloaded child pornography (charge dismissed for lack of evidence). All the allegations proved false but they served to distract the public from the real story – which was police incompetence. As long as the officer doing the smearing wasn't named he could say what he liked with no comeback.

This strategy of anonymous allegations was seen earlier, when the Metropolitan Police mistakenly shot Brazilian electrician Jean Charles de Menezes at Stockwell tube in July 2005. He was variously described by 'senior police sources' as running away from the police, jumping a tube barrier, wearing unusually bulky clothes in hot weather, and ignoring shouted warnings from the police. All these proved completely untrue.

As long as secrecy and anonymity reign, public sector bureaucracies will be the hiding places for the incompetent, lazy and corrupt. Failures will be rewarded and successes stifled. It's easier to lie when no one knows your name. It's easier to do all sorts of unethical, if not criminal, things when you are promised anonymity. Only by acting as a named individual and relating to others as such can there be justice and integrity in bureaucracies.

Throughout public services there are professionals with all kinds of information and concerns about what is not working and ideas for improvement. But in the current system they have nowhere to go, no one who will listen. In the end the silent state doesn't protect them, it slowly destroys their pride in their jobs and eventually their spirit to do good.

Public servants should be given the power over their own jobs and their accountability should be directly to the people, not to bureaucrats. Many currently have to sign confidentiality agreements, gagging them from speaking directly to the public in whose name and expense they are supposedly working. While they are silenced the top bureaucrats, such as Permanent Secretaries and deputy and undersecretaries, are not just implementing the decisions of ministers but taking the initiative in vast swathes of policymaking. Yet because of the quaint tradition of ministerial accountability and the convention on bureaucratic anonymity they are exempt from any kind of public accountability. Even at the lower level, there are important decisions being made and the public have a right to know who is making these decisions, particularly when they so directly affect their lives.

A system of named identification and direct accountability gives power back to the professionals. We don't need more targets or more bureaucratic inspectorates. We need knowledge, the raw data held inside our public services, to be given back to us. But as we'll see in the next chapter, the state no longer sees this as *our* information.

5

Pricing Us out of the Information Market

A basic principle of trade is that if you hand over money, you get something in return. That's how most markets work, but not, it transpires, the market of public information in the UK. In this marketplace you pay your taxes for information to be collected in your name, but may wind up paying twice, three times, sometimes eight times over to access data supposedly collected for public benefit. The restrictions and high price of most civic data hugely hamper our ability to understand and engage in society. How can we call ourselves an informed electorate when the state behaves like a robber baron of the 1900s, charging usurious rates as a result of an artificially maintained monopoly?

There is a new class divide between the information haves and have-nots; between the senior civil servants who are free to pore over pure unadulterated data and the rest of us who must either make do with the most paltry scraps of pre-processed information (such as a one-page fact sheet on knife crime) or pay a fortune for the good stuff (such as hospital admission data from the NHS Information Centre).

In a true democracy civic information belongs to the people and is free to use and reuse however one wishes. The state may have a monopoly on collecting information but it should not have a monopoly on its dissemination. Chances are you'll have heard of 'Crown copyright' (i.e. owned not by the people but by the Crown) but there are hundreds of similarly restrictive copyrights and they all mean one thing: that we – the supposed citizens in a democracy – must ask the state's permission to use public information. I know this may seem abstract, academic and maybe even a little dull. Who really cares about 'data'? But information is the lifeblood of power. He who controls it controls the agenda and thus other people, and if we want to be a free people, a free society, we must have free public information. This is all very worthy and principled but I find such arguments rarely persuade anyone, so instead I'm going to tell you a few stories. The first ones are about Parliament and relate the events that initially piqued my interest in this particular institution. The utter arrogance I encountered made me realise that these were people worthy of some *serious* investigation.

Looking down their noses at Up My Street

It was a call they'd been expecting and now it had come.

Tom Loosemore signalled for quiet in the grotty, sweaty Covent Garden office. The Aztec guys looked up from the new Douglas Adams PC game *Starship Titanic* they were writing. Next to Tom, his business partner Stefan Magdalinski came closer to listen in.

It was late September 1998 and from his window Tom looked over the ancient cobbled street of Maiden Lane into the private, first-floor dining room of Rules, one of London's snootiest restaurants. It epitomised the archaic establishment that Tom, Stef and their colleagues, who were all in their twenties, were fighting. Now they were about to engage directly with one of its emissaries – Her Majesty's Stationery Office.

Tom and Stef were prepared for the call. Their position: no compromise. If that meant the government would shut down their new civic website, so be it. They were confident that such a shutdown would prompt public outrage and kick-start the long-overdue information revolution that was being held back by the very government that kept proclaiming it was encouraging new technological enterprise.

Tom and Stef were developers who had been hired by Aztec Internet, a boutique IT consultancy, to build a website that would showcase the talents of the company's programmers. They were young and everything seemed possible. The duo had the idea of creating a one-stop shop for civic information which they named Up My Street. Simply by entering a postcode, users would be able to find out about schools in the neighbourhood, house prices, crime incidents, police clear-up rates, ambulance response times and the name of their local MP. They'd taken the precaution of writing to HMSO from the very outset, explaining their plan to mine various public websites for information, collect the data together and make it searchable to the public by postcode. The whole service would be free to users.

Eventually they'd received a reply from HMSO consisting of the most trenchant legalese. Its meaning was so unclear that Aztec's company lawyer, who'd been in the business for twenty years, couldn't tell whether HMSO were saying yes or no. It was so ambiguous, he advised, that the guys actually had a defensible position in court that they'd been given permission to develop the site, should a breach of copyright suit ever be filed. It was on this basis that Tom and Stef launched UpMyStreet.com.

But that was some time ago – and now they had a lawyer from HMSO on the phone. The woman spoke in a posh voice and was nice – for a lawyer.

'I've seen your site and what you've done. I'm guessing you don't have a licence for the information you're using. Do you know that you need one?'

Tom and Stef did know but they didn't think they should have to get a licence as the information was clearly in the public interest and, crucially, was already publicly available. It would have taken months to get all the necessary licences, and besides, Tom told the lawyer, they weren't even applicable to the Internet. They were based on an old-fashioned, print-only business model. Tom couldn't see a compromise. The law simply had to be changed to make public information freely available for the public to use.

'Would you like us to take the site down? Is that what you're asking?'

Tom and Stef had gone to a lot of effort to build Up My Street and by far the hardest part was simply getting official data off the poorly designed government websites and databases so they could make it usable. Ironically enough, the most difficult data to obtain was that which concerned the most people: school test results. It was the first year the Department of Education had published these results, but they were virtually unusable to members of the public. The department had given out the data to newspapers on a disk that was locked (meaning the data was static rather than dynamic and thus it couldn't be searched or analysed in any way, such as ranking schools), and there were no geographic locators so parents couldn't compare schools in the same area. Tom managed to get hold of a disk and tried to access the underlying data, but he found not only was the data locked but the bureaucrats had used an obscure proprietary format so the disk could only be read on a certain type of computer. To top it off, the local education authorities were listed on the disk only by a code, and when the guys asked the Department of Education for a key to the codes they were charged £1,000 for an A4 sheet of paper with the list.

'No one in their right mind would *ever* build a database that way,' Tom told me. He attributed the format to either massive incompetence or a determination 'to make it as difficult as possible for the public to see this information'. In the end, he had to get a hacker in Russia to reverse-engineer the disk and free the data. It was perhaps for this civic activism that the Department of Education took a dislike to the developers, even though they were making schools data more accessible to more parents, which, we should remember, was precisely what department officials claimed to want to do.

'All our attempts to be given access to the school results data (or attend the technical meetings) at the same time as the big national newspapers were ignored,' Stef said. He recalled seeing an email accidentally sent to him from an education official in which Up My Street was referred to as 'that stupid website'.

Back on the phone with the lawyer, Tom was hoping she'd bite and threaten to shut them down. She didn't.

'We want to help make the site legitimate,' she claimed.

Tom pointed out that technically they weren't abusing the terms of Crown copyright and that, far from corrupting the data, they were in fact correcting it. But that was irrelevant – simply the fact that a citizen was using official information without having a licence from government (e.g. asking permission) was the problem. 'We had no concept we were doing anything wrong,' Tom said. 'It's my data. I paid for it. It's about my government. If I'd corrupted it then I can see the government's concerns but we weren't doing that. We were making it more accessible and by making it so widely available we were improving the quality too as more people could scrutinise it.'

The lawyer eventually suggested that if Tom and Stef agreed not to release the data to anyone (yes, *anyone*) else they would be allowed to use it. So much for government rhetoric about empowering citizens! The guys agreed and Her Majesty's Stationery Office got off their back.

Aztec then folded and reformed as Upmystreet Ltd. They got venture capital and expanded. Great. Except the entire time they were building up the business they had to contend with the government constantly claiming that it might build an identical service (at taxpayer expense). Tony Blair announced the creation of Directgov, which was meant to be like Up My Street but never came close (and wasted countless millions in the process). Such pointlessness is perpetrated all across government, with various monopoly public bodies hoovering up vast quantities of taxpayer cash (e.g. Royal Mail, Ordnance Survey, Network Rail, Land Registry, etc.), all the while pretending they are businesses and charging taxpayers for the privilege of accessing information their taxes paid to create. This is ludicrous because the government is *not* a business. The whole point of paying taxes is to provide services for the common good for which there is no profit motive. While the state may be justified in having a monopoly on gathering public data (about crime incidents, laws passed, bills proposed, etc.), it is not justified in monopolising the *presentation* of that data. In 2010, a new website, data.gov.uk, was launched with the promise of offering better access to official data. While this is a step in the right direction, most of the data was already in the public domain, but the truly powerful data – such as postcodes, maps, company records, land holdings and meteorological data – are still off-limits. Even now officials refuse to release this public data to the citizenry at large. Instead, they will get taken out to some ritzy lunch by representatives of a private company which will then miraculously be awarded a contract to build a substandard IT system at vast public expense. The raw data will become the proprietorial possession of the private company and the public will be locked out for as long as the contract lasts. By contrast, releasing information to the public would cost nothing and would encourage innovations that would inevitably build up the country's tax base, as we'll see later in this chapter.

Hiding from their constituents

Tom and Stef discovered an interesting but shocking fact from their work on Up My Street: about half the country had no idea who their MP was. This gave them the idea for their next project: a website that told people, just by typing in a postcode, the name of their MP and a mechanism by which they could be contacted.

'This was our first experience of how fucked up British democracy was,' Tom said. 'We just couldn't believe this information wouldn't be available. What's not to like about people knowing who their MP is?'

But there was plenty parliamentary officials didn't like. For starters, no one in Parliament was remotely helpful in telling Tom and Stef who held the data needed to make such a site possible. When they did finally locate the person (the serjeant-at-arms) they found him far from enthusiastic. They realised that if they were going to build such a website, they would have to do so with no help (and a good deal of hindrance) from people paid to serve the public. They had tried official channels and (as any journalist could have told them) it had been a complete waste of time, so they resorted to the old-fashioned method – knowing the right people. Fortunately Tom did know some of the right people and through them he was able to get hold of the bible of political contacts – the BBC Blue Book, in which the contact details for MPs, Lords, MEPs and other senior political officials are printed.

'We got it in a brown bag like we were in some kind of spy movie,' Tom told me, 'and then had to set about manually transcribing it. That was the only way we could get MPs'' fax numbers if you can believe it. We certainly couldn't get them out of Parliament! We had long conversations with the serjeant-at-arms and he was adamant that the only number the public were getting was the main switchboard. The Lords is still like that.'

In 2000 the website Fax Your MP was born.

'The vast majority of MPs were supportive of our efforts up until we did league tables of their response rates to constituents and then they began complaining that what we were doing wasn't fair,' Tom said. 'We got comments from them like, "Why are you picking on us for taking two weeks to respond when that's the public sector norm?" Or, "Who gave you the right to compare us like this?"' Of course nobody gave them the right – and that's exactly as it should be in a democracy.

When emails began to replace faxes, the site was upgraded and became www.writetothem.com and included MEPs and local councillors. Parliament in its usual helpful manner refused to provide MPs' email addresses and so the developers were forced to fall back, yet again, on other sources. They managed to obtain a list of all MPs' official email addresses but many didn't work. Nor would Parliament provide them with photographs of MPs so they had to scrape the BBC website for images. Some MPs then had the gall to complain the photos weren't flattering enough!

What really steamed up the MPs, though, was the developers' next project: a website publishing and analysing MPs' voting records. This time the government lawyers weren't so nice.

They work for you (at least they're supposed to)

First, though, let me introduce Julian Todd, a computer programmer working in Liverpool. Julian was upset about the government's decision to invade Iraq and wanted to find out how his local MP, Louise Ellman, had voted on the decision to go to war. Ellman was parachuted into the safe Liverpool seat through an all-women shortlist and became an MP in 1997. Julian was amazed to find that nowhere was there a single record of her votes on this issue or any other. He spent hours locating in Hansard, the official record of Parliament, all the debates about Iraq and then trying to find all the division lists where MPs' votes are counted. Being a computer programmer, he quickly saw how the data could be automated, sorted and made searchable and thus useful to the populous. He suggested the idea of building a website to his friend and former colleague Francis Irving (another mathematician and computer programmer) who'd just returned from a six-month backpacking trip around Asia.

'I wrote the first version of Public Whip in a month,' Francis told me. 'I was into it.' This is what I mean when I talk about innovation by the general public and why it should not be stifled, least of all by the government. Who could predict that someone with a first-class degree in mathematics from Oxford University would be interested in building a website that allows people to see how their MP voted? Yet that's exactly what happened. And at no cost to the public purse. Francis scraped the data from Hansard and put it into the new website called Public Whip (www.publicwhip.org.uk) so that each MP had a page where his or her votes were collected along with overall votes on selected topics of public interest – such as transparency of Parliament, ID cards, the Iraq War, etc. Using the site, Julian discovered his MP had voted very strongly for the Iraq War.

'People were quite amazed because it wasn't that common then to take official information and do something with it,' Francis said. 'And the computer people were surprised too because they hadn't really thought about applying their skills to politics or official information. The response from the computer community was tremendously positive.'

The reaction from parliamentarians was quite the opposite. While there was some communication in the early days between the developers and parliamentary officials (for example when Francis or Julian would find a mistake in the official record, such as someone shown as voting when they were, in fact, dead), mostly they were ignored. If you thought they might be thanked for providing this valuable public service at no cost, you'd be sadly mistaken.

Completely coincidentally, Tom and Stef wanted to create TheyWorkForYou.com, a one-stop shop for citizens about MPs and Lords. Francis had been in touch with Tom to ask about the postcode look-up from the Fax Your MP site and when Tom saw Public Whip they all realised how much they had in common and decided to join forces. A charity was created – mySociety – with the ethos of building civic websites.

Francis had built Public Whip simply by scraping (or 'nicking') Hansard. Tom wanted to get a regular feed direct from Parliament, but no one in Parliament knew much about the raw record as it was handled by the privatised arm of HMSO, the Stationery Office. It was not in the

Stationery Office's interest to help any outsider access the official record of Parliament as it had (and still has) a very cosy monopoly, publishing both the written and online record of Parliament in return for a hefty amount of public cash. As we'll see in the next chapter on courts, this is not at all unusual, even though it makes absolutely no sense for a public body to subsidise and grant a monopoly to a private company to distribute public information. It gives that company the unique ability to charge what it likes for civic data, without any pressure to innovate. Because of all this, Tom also had to scrape the online version of Hansard, which presented its own difficulties as the formatting was very poor.

'It was a mess. It needed to be a relational database but it wasn't. That was probably one of our biggest achievements – taking that piece of shit and making it an actual usable website.'

Tom hired Francis Irving and another programmer to build the site, based on an improved version of the Public Whip scraper. They showed a demo to parliamentary clerks and no one seemed to have a problem. When they launched a test version of the site, however, suddenly all hell broke loose.

'MPs complained about the name – they thought it was too aggressive. Then they said: "How do we know it's accurate?"'

We'll hear this argument again. Tom countered, asking how did they know Dod's (a parliamentary directory published by a private company) was accurate, or how any other big company publication that used parliamentary data could be trusted. That's how it is in the UK – if you're a big company and you play by the officials' rules then you get the info; if you're independent and refuse to cede control then you don't. If you're rich enough you can find out all you want about Parliament, but until mySociety came along, no one was publishing information for the general public. Why? Because there was no money in it and government officials were perfectly happy for the citizenry to remain ignorant.

Why do the mySociety guys do it?

I know them so I can tell you. Julian Todd does it because he's very worried about the state of the world. Francis Irving and most of the other mySociety 'geeks' cite the sheer fun of it, the satisfaction of achieving an aesthetic of usability. Francis describes the motivation thus:

'You look at a bad website and think how it could be so much better and how much easier it could make people's lives. I'm thinking that all the time whenever I see data. I look at the train ticket website, for example. Awful! I can see how it could be so much better. Matthew Somerville [another mySociety developer who's involved with They Work For You] built Accessible Odeon because he couldn't bear how they'd built a site that was only accessible on one type of browser. And rather than say "That's great and can we get you in as a consultant?" they made him shut it down. It's the same with transport timetables: train and bus. We've built all sorts of amazing products but because this is all weirdly private data we can't publish it. There are loads of things people could do and yet all the time the people in power are stopping us.'

At that time, Parliamentary copyright stated that you could do nothing with Hansard apart from download it for personal use. Tom, Francis and the others got a lot of blustery emails from MPs.

'The thing they hated most was voting records, particularly about Iraq,' Tom said. 'The whips had basically gone to town on that issue and every Labour MP was under extreme pressure to toe the government line. Most of them did, but they didn't want the public finding out! I absolutely lost it with an MP finally. It was another moan of "it's not fair". I said: "How can we make it better?" I genuinely wanted to know, but he had absolutely no suggestions and didn't even appear interested in improvement. He just wanted us to go away. There was no sense of this being a collaborative effort between the electorate and those they elect. He didn't get that *at all*. Eventually I had to put to him my old chestnut: "Do you want it taken down? Is that what you're saying?" Oh no! Of course not. Bluster bluster.'

MPs also didn't like their attendance records being published. That too, they claimed, wasn't fair because often they weren't on the floor but were in committee. But they refused to publish the committee attendance records so there was no way to confirm this.

Then in the summer of 2004, the Clerk of the Scrolls wrote a letter threatening the developers with legal action for breach of copyright. mySociety argued the only thing They Work For You did besides republishing existing information was aggregating votes. Did Parliament really want to sue a group of Web developers for allowing the public to know how MPs voted? It would have been a PR disaster (though I can tell you from personal experience that creating PR disasters is precisely what parliamentary officials do best).

Tom took the same approach: he refused to back down. Wiser heads in Parliament prevailed and the decision was made *not* to sue. A licence was granted. But that was not the end of their troubles. They had another problem: England's atrocious libel laws.

While Parliament has immunity from its own libel law (par for the course), it refused to transfer parliamentary privilege to They Work For You despite the fact it was republishing the direct record from Hansard. That saddled the developers with enormous financial risk. Indeed there was an instance where Hansard got it wrong, naming someone as a convicted criminal when they were in fact innocent. This person threatened Hansard but when he couldn't get any joy there he threatened They Work For You. Fortunately it just so happened that Theresa May MP knew of the developers' troubles and asked the minister Jack Straw if he could confirm that the site, as a reproducer of the parliamentary record, was covered by parliamentary privilege. He agreed and that was that. (Never forget – it's all about who you know!)

What we have, then, is two years (and vast amounts of public money) spent coming up with an Internet-use licence that made it somewhat easier and cheaper for the public to use public information. It would have been better simply to free the data, but it's the lack of control these officials can't stand.

The latest episode of this sorry saga concerns the broadcast footage of our Parliament. A cartel of broadcasters manages this in cooperation with Parliament, but to buy footage costs £20 per tape and you have to sign a contract that you won't use it for satirical purposes. Why not take this footage, chop it up and match it to the official written record?

'We got the footage from the BBC. We had volunteers willing to do it and they began. That's when you start to realise the official record and what is actually said don't always match up,' Tom told me. 'We were again called by the government lawyers. "You don't have a licence for this footage. It's Crown copyright."'

Isn't this becoming a bit farcical? You'd have thought by now these dinosaurs would have accepted the technological revolution (or at least the twenty-first century) but no, they were refusing to evolve. Tom told them the footage was in fact covered by Parliamentary copyright, not Crown copyright, which only covers the written record – Hansard – and not broadcast. It transpired the footage was a legal no-man's-land so mySociety was able to circumvent the system and get away with it.

Let's recall that these people aren't criminals. I am frankly amazed how Tom and the mySociety developers managed to keep their cool with such petulant jobsworths. They should be knighted for their services to constituents everywhere. If not for them the British public would still have little to no idea of how to contact their MPs, how they'd voted and their attendance in Parliament.

Yet look at all the ludicrous legal harassment they faced. Public servants must accept that in a democracy official information belongs to the people – not politicians, not civil servants, not the monarchy. In the UK, the government is doing its level best to stifle all IT innovation by sticking to an old-fashioned proprietary business model that treats civic information as a moneymaking widget.

A royal pain: shutting down civic society, one website at a time

I mentioned earlier that one of the things Tom and Stef discovered when they were building Fax Your MP was how few people knew the name of their Members of Parliament. They remedied this by providing a postcode look-up service so you could enter your postcode and the site would determine your MP. That makes it all sound easy – but getting hold of the postcodes was anything but simple.

Postcodes were developed in the 1950s at the Post Office Research Station in north London and rolled out over the next fifteen years by the Post Office. The codes enable letters to be read by electronic sorting machines for greater efficiency, and it was for this reason public money was spent, first developing the postcode system and then persuading the public to accept it. In return for our adoption of a code which makes life easier for the Post Office, the public are now denied access to the database their taxes paid to create and promote. Whether you're a direct-mail marketing company, a non-profit pro-democracy group, charity or citizen – you'll be charged at least £4,000 annually for the collected list of all postcodes. What follows are just a few examples of the Great Postcode Robbery.

When Tom and Stef were creating Up My Street in 1998, Royal Mail was just beginning to think about how it could charge the public for public information. The guys wanted postcodes for the look-up service but not the entire data set of every single mailing address (the Postcode Address File), just a thin slice of civic data – about 1.6 million postcodes out of some 28 million addresses. The data changes frequently so quarterly updates are needed. Initially Royal Mail sold them the data for a single-use fee but then in 2000/1 it began demanding thousands of pounds.

Bear in mind that the Royal Mail doesn't even collect postcode data. It is local councils (funded by the taxpaying public) who do the hard work of gathering, compiling and correcting the addresses and postcodes in their area. They then hand over this data to Royal Mail who compile it and then, gallingly, *sell it back* to the councils (so the public is already paying twice for the same information and if they want individual access they'll be paying yet again). Technically the charge is for 'added value' but the efforts made by Royal Mail are minimal at best. While it might seemingly be right to charge a direct-mail company hoping to make lots of money from the data set, the same business model applies to *all* types of organisations. In fact, charities are the Royal Mail's biggest customer for the postcode database. The only reason civic websites like They Work For You can continue to operate is because they have been granted special dispensation and fall under the government's special licence. Other start-ups or voluntary organisations have no such protection from the short-term usurious greed of the Royal Mail's management.[1]

One of these is the website www.ernestmarples.com. Named after the postmaster general who first introduced the postcode, this site was created in 2009 by developer Richard Pope with his friend Harry Metcalfe. They knew just how useful the postcode look-up facility was for all sorts

1. Royal Mail Holdings plc is a 'company' in which the government (i.e. the public) own 100 per cent of its shares.

of socially beneficial projects, but because Royal Mail charges so much for it, these non-profits had to spend countless laborious hours scraping postcode information from all across the Web. Richard and Harry decided to write a program that automated this scraping and made it easier for all these voluntary sites to use postcode info. They didn't charge for it but did set themselves up as a limited company just in case the Royal Mail tried to sue them. Within weeks, all sorts of websites were using the service provided by ernestmarples.com, including:

- Jobcentre Pro Plus – to search for jobs in your area
- PlanningAlerts.com – alerts of planning applications near you
- The Straight Choice – to monitor the claims of election leaflets
- voteUK – a mobile service to look up your local polling station
- LiveBus – real-time bus updates for your area
- The National Greasy Caff Database – find your nearest greasy hangover cure
- UK OnScreen – discover the locations of movie scenes shot in the UK
- HealthWhere – find your nearest hospitals and pharmacies

All was quiet for three months – and why not? It's not like these intelligent, civically active young men were criminals; quite the opposite. They weren't stealing – not even from Royal Mail – as all the data they'd collected was from publicly available websites. Yet postcodes in their collected form (no matter how you get them) are 'owned' by Royal Mail. Just to be clear, the developers made no money from the site and all the effort building it was done by unpaid volunteers.

On 2 October 2009 Richard and Harry got a rather nasty letter from law firm CMS Cameron McKenna threatening not just the limited company they'd set up to protect themselves but each of them individually. It should be noted this was the first and only communication they'd had from Royal Mail. Their options were stark: either they shut down the website or face a costly legal battle. They were just two young guys with not much money and they were in no position to mount an effective legal challenge. Their cause was clearly in the public interest but the public's money was subsidising the side seeking to stop the public accessing information their taxes had paid for! Figure that one out.

Reluctantly, Richard and Harry shut down their site – another victory for the short-term greed of our so-called public institutions. Immediately, all the sites using the free ernestmarples.com data went down too. So no more HealthWhere, Jobcentre Pro Plus and PlanningAlerts.com. Users from property developers to community bloggers were affected. Even Lincoln City Council was using ernestmarples data because it was easier and more accessible then that provided by Royal Mail, so part of the city website went down. This is the lunacy of the current business model where one part of the state takes down another, all over a proprietorial battle for information paid for by the public.

'We thought we'd found a way around what is a real problem in the UK,' Richard told me. 'If you want to locate anything in this country from a bus stop to a planning application, you need to use a postcode which tells you where in the world it is located. Yell.com is paying £4,000 a year per computer to license this data gathered at taxpayer expense. If you're a Google or Tesco then that's fine, you can afford it, but if you're a citizen or a non-profit or a start-up company there's no way you can pay £4,000 upfront.'

It leaves one wondering: how many Googles has our own government killed because of its short-term, petty, bureaucratic control freakery? How many start-ups have been forced out of business that could have added huge amounts to the country's tax base? All because the Royal Mail sits on the postcode database like a dragon on its pot of gold.

'We've probably got the best geocoding system in the world,' Richard says. 'We should have spawned this amazing geolocation industry in the UK as a result, but it's been stifled because of the Royal Mail's attitude.'

It's not just do-gooders being stifled but business entrepreneurs who are crucial for revitalising the economy. 192.com was a small start-up when it was threatened by Royal Mail for £300 million for copyright and licensing breaches related to postcode data. The owner had to endure two years of legal battles that only ended when he won in the High Court. In 2002 CEO Alastair Crawford was building a business that made accessible and searchable various so-called public records such as electoral rolls, company registrations, land transactions and telephone directories. His team began by collecting electoral registers from more than 350 different councils. Big credit companies such as Equifax and Experian already had access to the registers and had collated them digitally, but they were refusing to grant licences to anyone outside their reseller group and as such they had a monopoly on this public information thanks to the government's policy of forbidding general public access to this public information. This was done under the guise of 'protecting our privacy', which I discuss in Chapter 7. In the absence of licences, 192.com had to go around the country collecting paper copies of the electoral registers and then send all the copies to China where the information was entered digitally. All this needless effort when the registers existed in digital form initially! Here is the lifecycle of the electoral roll:

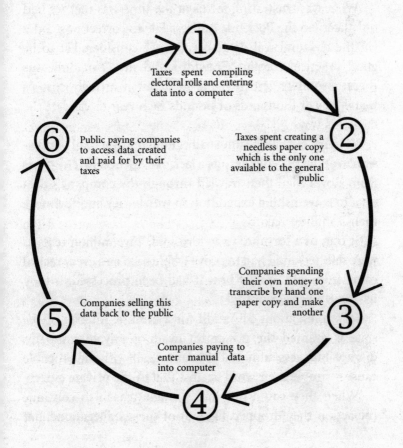

① Taxes spent compiling electoral rolls and entering data into a computer

② Taxes spent creating a needless paper copy which is the only one available to the general public

③ Companies spending their own money to transcribe by hand one paper copy and make another

④ Companies paying to enter manual data into computer

⑤ Companies selling this data back to the public

⑥ Public paying companies to access data created and paid for by their taxes

It was only after doing all this that the credit companies agreed to offer licences for the material they held. So how does Royal Mail fit into this?

A large part of the electoral register is addresses. Many of these addresses have incorrect or incomplete postcodes and 192.com corrected the postcodes using a postcode validation tool under licence from Royal Mail. Royal Mail objected to that process, claiming 192.com had violated a clause in the postcode licensing agreement.

'What was frustrating for us at the time was that we had only licensed the Postcode Address File to correct postcodes [in the electoral roll data] because we considered it to be good practice,' Alastair Crawford told me. 'Not only was there absolutely zero revenue in it but it actually cost us many tens of thousands of pounds each year to validate the data this way.'

A High Court judge unusually granted Royal Mail permission to audit 192.com despite a lack of evidence. Investigators from Royal Mail then trawled through the company's data on a massive fishing expedition in which they audited more than 5 million records.

'It cost us a fortune,' Crawford said. 'Five million records were selected and I had to prove where each and every record came from and exactly how it had been processed. It took us about twelve months.'

Let's think about this audit for a minute. An arm of the state is granted the power to invade a private company, disrupt business, almost bankrupt it, all without probable cause – simply their word against that of the private citizen.

'When they could not find a single reason to continue the action they dropped five out of the six allegations, but not until we had spent £1 million defending it, and not until the last day of trial,' Crawford said.

With just the remaining question of interpretation of Royal Mail's own licence agreement, the court ruled in 192.com's favour but decided to go against convention by refusing to grant full costs on an indemnity basis. Shortly afterwards Royal Mail replaced the two managers of the Royal Mail Address Management and apologised to 192.com. Since then 192.com has traded without interference. But it cost them £1 million and a High Court victory to do so. No wonder Richard Pope and Harry Metcalfe decided to shut down their website.

The situation is no better when it comes to a more graphical look at where in the world we are.

The usual BS from OS

Ordnance Survey is the nation's mapping agency and for the majority of its life it was wholly funded by the taxpayer. Nowadays if you want the fruits of that labour you have to pay. To pour salt in the wound, your taxes are also spent by OS to take legal action against members of the public who dare to make maps available to their fellow citizens.

Andy Wightman wanted to produce the definitive account of who owns Scotland. He's a freelance writer and researcher specialising in Scottish land issues and director of the Caledonia Centre for Social Development. In 1996 he wrote a book, *Who Owns Scotland*, which detailed over 1,500 land-holdings (about 70 per cent of Scotland's land area). When he was considering updating the book, he thought a live, digitised version on the Internet would be the best way to make the data public, so in 2000 he created some test web pages. After receiving a positive response, he raised enough money to begin the laborious process of researching all Scottish landholdings from the raw title deeds held in the National Archives of Scotland and recorded by the Register of Scotland. It was a slow and time-consuming process but it meant the data was far more accurate than ever before. Andy worked on the site for more than four years on a mostly unpaid basis.

An essential part of illustrating land boundaries is to provide a map over which the boundaries are drawn. Unfortunately, in the UK, Ordnance Survey has a virtual monopoly on geographic data and it is Crown copyright. While the OS has always been a public body paid for by the public because it is deemed to produce a public good, since 1999 it has operated as a trading fund – a New Labour creation whereby a public body pretends it is a private company. But unlike a private company it was built by the taxpayer, subsidised by the taxpayer and operates in a monopoly marketplace, all the while charging the taxpayer for the information it created in the name of the public.

In the usual way, Andy's main obstacle to creating this innovative website was the UK government itself. 'The only constraint to implementing our ideal solution for the display of land-ownership records was the expense of OS mapping data,' he told me. 'This project was being run as a not-for-profit educational and research exercise and at the time we had no funds other than our own very limited personal resources. Visitors to the website wouldn't pay to access the information, nevertheless OS said we would need a business-user licence. As a concession they said because the data would be on just one PC, we would only have to pay for a single-user licence.'

Even at this vastly reduced rate, Andy was still paying just over £2,500 for the maps he needed. Much of Scotland is covered in forest, and Andy's next step was to contact the Forestry Commission to get their digital landholding records. The commission was happy to oblige but they, too, faced issues with Ordnance Survey who were claiming copyright over the maps of Forestry Commission land. Is this all starting to sound rather Kafkaesque? Wait, oh wait! It gets worse.

The question of the Forestry Commission land brought Andy's project once again to the attention of OS and a public servant then thought it worth his while to examine the site and wrote to Andy complaining that the maps were not properly watermarked. So Andy had to spend several months manually manipulating each image to include an acceptable watermark. The OS seemed satisfied and laid off him for a while.

Things got truly bizarre in October 2004 when Andy received a letter from Chris Lewis, of Ordnance Survey's intellectual property team, stating that 'Your reproduction of Ordnance Survey mapping/data on the website without our authorisation or a licence is an infringement of Crown copyright in accordance with the Act.' This came as a shock since by then Andy had paid OS a total of £4,371 for licences and had a written agreement with them to do exactly what he was doing. He assumed there must have been a communications breakdown between the licensing and copyright divisions. He phoned up and, after talking with officials, received another email confirming what he knew already, namely that he *did* have a licence and *was* allowed to use the maps.

All went quiet again and the following spring Andy was ready to consider a second edition of his book. He wrote to OS in February 2005 asking them about the licensing conditions if he were to distribute his website on a CD-ROM along with the next edition of *Who Owns Scotland*. In April he was called by a Mr Santi Jago who told him they would need to meet. This was followed by a letter on 23 May 2005 from Philip Lines, head of OS's Partner Team, in which the OS were suddenly claiming that 'the website is not in compliance with clause 3.1 of our Framework Direct Licence (FDL)' despite the OS granting precisely this permission eight months earlier.

Andy was left bewildered and alarmed at the way OS kept changing the rules every six months and their increasing avariciousness in demanding ever more money.

'As I made inquiries I became more confused by OS licensing arrangements and shocked at how much I was going to have to pay if I was to continue operating as I had been doing in the full knowledge of OS and with their agreement since early 2002.'

Even more frighteningly, the new demands made by the OS were never pinned down to an exact financial amount, which left him with no choice but to remove the OS maps.

From what he could gather, the new arrangement meant a hike from £789.60 in 2005 to between £10,000 and £15,000 for the first year with further annual payments of between £5,000 and £10,000. No business could behave this way in the private sector. They would be driven out by a competitor within months. That is the great fallacy of the 'trading fund'. With research costs spiralling as a result of increased access costs, he decided it was no longer sustainable to operate the site as a public good and changed the site so users must pay an annual subscription of £10 to view the data.

If you're not incredulous enough by reading all that: since August 2007 Ordnance Survey has spent at least £42,076 plus VAT paying a political lobbying company, Mandate Communications, to lobby politicians to stop the public being able to freely access mapping data. Your taxes hard at work to stop you seeing where you live.

One final example for anyone still doubting the restrictive effect of Crown copyright comes from a reader of my blog. He'd requested a map from Cambridge City Council of the electoral boundaries of his voting district. The council wrote back to say they could not supply an electronic version of the map because of Ordnance Survey's copyright restrictions. In addition, the requester was told that the hard copy of the map supplied was for his sole use and that he could not share it with the public.

What sort of nonsense is it when the public are not even allowed access to maps of their own electoral boundaries?! Our taxes paid for the creation of the Ordnance Survey and through our council tax we pay again so that councils can access this public data. As if that's not silly enough, we are then told we have to pay again if we want to publish maps of our voting wards. OS has made a small concession and agreed that some electoral maps can be used but only on acceptance of their highly restrictive *terms and conditions*. We should not need the 'kind permission' of the Ordnance Survey to use information that our taxes have already paid for, especially when it is fundamental to the democratic process.

Imagine if the private sector worked this way. An entrepreneur (in this case the state) decides to map Britain, so he goes to investors (the taxpaying public) and gets £50 million to cover the costs of creating this business. Having spent that money but deciding to grow the business anyway, he looks to a second investor (licence-fee payers) for a further £5 million. If this were a real company the investor recoup would look something like this:

Initial investor: 60%
Entrepreneur: 35%
Second-round investor: 5%

This is as it should be, as the initial investor (the venture capitalist if you will) is putting up the most money and, crucially, carrying the most risk, while the secondary investor has put in little and carries little risk. In Britain's ludicrously short-sighted system this is completely subverted to screw the public and the recoup on investment is as follows:

Entrepreneur: 51%
Second-round investor: 49%
Initial investor: 0%

So the public gets precisely nothing for all the money put in and risk taken while the government keeps total control over a supposedly public product (such as maps, postcodes, Companies House filings, tidal charts, land registrations, parliamentary debates, weather charts . . . the list is long) and access is given instead only to the second-round investor who can afford to buy the product for commercial exploit subject to constant government oversight and interference.

Google was started by two guys in a garage. If they'd had to pay or get a licence to access every site on the Internet or for every terminal on which the data was stored they could never have afforded to grow their business. The reason they could is because in the United States public information belongs not to the Crown but the people; it must be provided free or at little cost and federal law states any text produced by government is free from copyright and passes immediately into the public domain. Unoriginal compilations of fact – public or private – may not be owned, Professor James Boyle of Duke Law School told me. He's studied copyright regimes in the US and Europe and says despite its reputation as the heart of capitalism, the US government exercises 'information socialism', whereas the UK and the rest of Europe are out for maximum short-term profit at the expense of social welfare and long-term economic growth.

Rufus Pollock, of the Open Knowledge Foundation, cites the $500 million, copyright-free US weather data industry as the reason why the US weather risk-management sector is ten times larger than the European one. Charles Arthur, the *Guardian*'s technology editor, credits the rise of the multibillion-dollar satnav industry to the free GPS data provided by the US government. 'This data is used worldwide, and it has generated a huge industry from electronics companies making the components to navigational software systems plus all the things you don't see such as greater productivity because people no longer get lost. Then look at how Europe, in its genius, reacted. It spent tax money building a rival system which is fully encrypted so you have to pay to access it. Surprise, surprise, people prefer the free GPS system.'

Free public data means more jobs, with more people producing more valuable products, generating more social wealth. So why does the British government refuse to shift from its archaic position? It's the 'jam today' philosophy where two pence today is worth (in the minds of civil servants) more than a pound in the future.

'OS is never going to be a billion-pound business,' Charles Arthur says, 'whereas Google is. No matter how much you try and push postcode data, Royal Mail is never going to grow that big because people can't afford to pay that licence. If you take away the fee then the sky's the limit.'

We will never see the likes of a British Google while the entire establishment is hell-bent on stifling the entrepreneurial spirit of this country's finest geeks and innovators. It's that old attitude again: never trust the public – and it seems to me identical to the reaction of elites back in the 1870s and 80s to the universal Education Acts. Back then, the powerful were outraged because they felt education was the privilege of the elites, and the masses couldn't be trusted to read or write. How is this any different from the attitude of the Royal Mail today? Of Ordnance Survey or our very own Parliament? And perhaps the place where this elitist view is most prevalent is where we most expect to see justice – the courts.

6

Secret Justice

Justice must be seen to be done. That's the famous aphorism stated most succinctly in 1924 by Chief Justice Lord Hewart.[1] But what happens when you put the rhetoric to the test and try and see some actual justice being done? That is what I set out to do in this chapter. If you've been in a court you'll know what it's like, but I want to delve right into the depths of the court service. I have done my utmost to drag Parliament into the modern democratic age and it seems the next institution in need of such a makeover is the courts.

There are three main things the public need to know about courts:

1. who is using them
2. for what purpose (e.g. the case detail)
3. the result

1. The judge stated: 'It is not merely of some importance but is of fundamental importance that justice should not only be done, but should manifestly and undoubtedly be seen to be done.'

We need to know these things to ensure justice is being done, to understand the laws under which we live and to make best use of the finite resources that fund the judicial system. If the courts are becoming the preserve of the rich, corrupt or brutal, then we need to know as we are footing the bill. Such an allegation is currently levelled at the High Court, which has become the epicentre of 'libel tourism' whereby wealthy businessmen, medical companies and even suspected terrorists from around the globe use the English courts to suppress stories they don't like.

Overall, our court service cost us £1.48 billion in 2008/9, up from £1.3 billion in 2007/8 (a 13.8 per cent increase). Civil courts make up £408 million of that, family courts £196 million and the remainder goes to the criminal courts. In addition, we pay £2.1 billion in legal aid costs, yet the records from these cases are not available to the public. Total staff costs are £859 million, of which £284 million goes to judges. Senior judges are paid a total of £180 million, of which 491 are judicial officers and 281 full-time-equivalent district judges (paid by the day). Salaries for a further 956 members of the senior judiciary are met from the consolidated fund, i.e. off-budget, so these headline figures don't even cover the full costs.

We pay a lot for our court system, but to be honest, it's not enough. Courts are under-resourced, there aren't as many as there need to be to meet demand, and facilities are in desperate need of modernisation. Open justice should be honoured as a point of principle, but if we're going to invest even more public money in the court system it's vital we understand where this money is going and receive some benefit for our considerable contribution. You might think there would be a drive in the judiciary to enable citizens to access the justice system in the easiest manner possible, for example without having to come to court, but that is not the case. Quite the opposite drive exists. Those few people who attend court either individually or on behalf of the public face a barrage of obscure, illogical and mercurially enforced rules. Trying to obtain court documents is about as easy and affordable as circumnavigating the globe. What this shows is the complete lack of regard within the judicial system for the public's right to see justice being done. It is an afterthought, and very often not even that. There is simply no understanding that the courts exist solely for the interests of the public at large. And if the public can't see justice being done then the entire system is little more than a cloistered club solely for the benefit of judges, lawyers and their lackeys, a sort of care in the community for the upper-middle classes and their servants.

Some courts have dragged themselves into the twenty-first century and are equipped with modern technology (microphones to amplify the main participants and TV screens for CCTV footage or satellite link-ups), but the representation of the courtroom itself remains thoroughly nineteenth century. Back then, of course, the way people saw justice being done was to go along to their local court and sit through a trial. Before television or the Internet, trials were the ultimate reality entertainment, revealing all the riches (and horrors) of humanity. I'm not a fan of so-called reality TV – if I want reality, I get it the old-fashioned way and go along to the public gallery of a local court. Let's head to one now.

Courtroom drama

'Defend the children of the poor and punish the wrongdoer'

These are the words atop one of the most famous courts in the world: the Central Criminal Court, or Old Bailey as it's commonly known. On a drizzly grey day in November this is where I am, standing outside the imposing columns of the Victorian court edifice. The main entrance is glorious, with the sculpted curves of robed women and, high above, the golden statue of Justice herself. But here at the main gate a black metal portcullis bars entry and, I'm told, is opened only for ceremonial occasions. Abutting the ornate stately court building is a brutalist extension expressing that void of taste so indicative of the 1970s. It's here that you find the main entrance for the press, lawyers, court staff and others appearing in court. But not, it transpires, the public. Usually I attend as a member of the press and as such use my press card to enter the court precinct. Today, though, I am here as a common Joe, a mere member of the public (only the person footing the bill for all this!), so I'll have to forgo the friendly security guard cosseted behind bullet-proof glass and instead make my way further down the street to the public-gallery entrance.

There's nothing inherently wrong with separating the public from the main courtroom provided the facilities are 'separate but equal', but I'm getting the distinct impression that's not going to be the case as I arrive at Warwick Passage, a grotty alleyway strewn with rubbish some yards down from the main entrance. It looks like the servants' or trade entrance, though to be fair at least servants could take their belongings with them. For the public the list of contraband items is extensive: no cameras, phones, cassette or CD players, bags or holdalls, radios, pagers, food or drink (which explains all the dumped Tesco bags filled with food).

The walls are plastered with hectoring notices: 'Public gallery conditions of entry: persons declining to be searched will be refused access', 'Photography of any kind is prohibited within the precinct of the court building. It is an offence to take or publish such images under section 41 of the Criminal Justice Act 1925 and may be treated as Contempt of Court.'

They become increasingly indignant: 'ALSO NOTE THAT THERE IS NO WHEELCHAIR ACCESS TO THE BUILDING. NO FOOD OR DRINK ALLOWED. NO WRITING MATERIAL ALLOWED.' (No writing material? This is news to me.)

I head up a narrow staircase surrounded by chartreuse walls to a guard waiting beside a metal detector. He says no phones or large bags allowed. What about writing? Can I take in my notepad? He says I can but there is no storage for the forbidden items such as my phone. He says there is a sandwich shop across the road or a bar further along the street where I can leave the items for a charge.

I fall into conversation with Murat Mert, the owner of Bailey's Sandwich Bar. He inherited the bag/phone-storage trade from the previous owner and charges £1 for phones, £2 for bags. The business isn't what it was, he says. 'A couple of years ago there were full sittings. Not any more.' On the day I visit he is storing just two phones. It seems the courts' efforts to discourage the public from seeing justice is working.

I ask him if he's ever been into the public galleries of the Old Bailey. He hasn't. 'Why don't you come with me?' He says he will and hands over the running of the shop to his colleague.

'One at a time please,' the guard tells us sternly back at the top of the staircase. Murat waits while I hand over my pen, notebook and wallet for inspection then step through a metal detector. We go up to the first floor where we are greeted by yet another hectoring sign: 'It is a criminal offence to take photographs or video clips in court – whether with a camera, mobile phone or video recorder or any other device.' Then in BOLD RED: 'You could be sent to prison for up to two years.' Such bullying signs serve to make the citizen feel like a criminal, fearful of doing anything wrong. He is not treated as though he has a right to be here; instead, he is here under sufferance and if he makes one wrong move he'll be tossed in the clink. As we enter the first floor the security guard smiles broadly. Turns out he's a regular of the sandwich shop. 'What are you doing here?' he asks Murat. He's friendly, which is a good thing, because it's the guards and the ushers who know about the cases. Public courts will list the names of cases to be heard on the day but these don't tell you anything other than the name (usually not even the full name) of the parties involved. Going into a trial without the accompanying documents or case background is like rocking up to a film halfway through – you've no idea what's going on. The listing officers will usually have brief summaries of the cases, and in criminal courts the time of the offence and some specifics, but these are not made public. This means court sketchers and reporters who must cover dozens of trials simultaneously are heavily reliant on court staff to give them a heads-up on what cases are of interest. It's another patronage system, with the public having no statutory right to information that is supposedly 'public'; instead, they must rely on knowing the right people and keeping chummy with them. In our case it's thanks to Murat that the guard is happy to share details about the trials on his floor. There's a murder trial going on in court 14 which he tells us about; we decide to sit in on that. Another officer at a small desk looks at my notebook suspiciously. 'You're not going to be taking notes, are you?'

'Yes, I'd planned on it,' I say.

'You can't be doing that.'

'Why not?'

'Judge's order.'

'What sort of order?' He seems taken aback that I'm asking for a justification as to why I can't record what's happening in a supposedly open court. 'Judge's order,' he repeats. I turn to the security guard, who helpfully explains that because the trial involves teenagers there is a section 39 order in place granting the juveniles anonymity. I still don't see why that precludes the public taking notes – surely if anyone wanted to they would simply do what court sketchers routinely resort to and write from memory outside. It seems logic is in short supply when it comes to public access of the courts.

'You'll be in serious trouble if you start taking notes,' the officer stresses. 'The judge takes a very dim view of that.'

'Is he going to confiscate my notebook?'

'No, but whatever you do, don't open it!' he says. 'And hide your pen.'

This all seems farcical but I follow his instruction and

tuck the contraband pen into my pocket. An usher lets us into the gallery (later, when I want to leave, I have to tap him on the knee to wake him up).[2] Once we're seated I look around at my fellow court twitchers. This trial is the only one happening this afternoon on this floor yet it's not packed. I count just thirteen people including myself. What I also notice is the view (occluded) and the seats (uncomfortable). The importance of each person in this hierarchy is made clear by the seat upon which his or her bottom rests. So the judge has a high-backed green leather chair embossed with a gold crest. Below him, the lawyers nestle their robed posteriors on comfy green fabric chairs with brushed blonde arms, as do the jurors. Those in the dock sit on an inferior version of the fabric chair while the press must make do with hard, black plastic fold-down seats. These are the same seats we have in the public galleries. (We may be paying for this theatre but we're definitely getting the cheap seats.) The view is obstructed in most galleries so only those in the front row can see all the participants and even then they must lean forward onto the metal railing to see the witnesses giving testimony, a posture which usually earns them a stern telling-off from the usher (when awake).

It was not always like this.

Go into one of the original courtrooms – say court 1 or 2, built at the turn of the last century – and you'll see how the public were once centre stage; the gallery open, spacious and right in the middle of the action. These original courtrooms are spaces of great beauty, temples of justice that look

2. Court staffers seem to need a lot of sleep. Near the press room of the Old Bailey is a staffroom, and when I take a look inside one morning at 10 o'clock, I find five staffers fast asleep on sofas.

like a mini chamber of the House of Commons. The press box was row upon row of polished wood, and across the tiled hall from the court, the original press room, another beautiful space with a spiral staircase and windows looking out onto the street. There seems to have been a real appreciation back then of the importance of both the press and the public, whereas today's courts push the public into garret-like galleries and the press into a windowless basement hovel.

Murat and I watch from our eyrie the trial of teenage girls accused of murdering another teenage girl by forcing her out of a tower-block window to her death. But with no material telling us about the case (where we are in the trial, who's who, etc.) we grow weary and leave. I reflect that this is a public building, and in the case of the Old Bailey, the public is usually funding the costs for *both* sides through legal aid. Another trial upstairs comprises thirteen wigged lawyers for half a dozen defendants. I'm told the average cost of a criminal trial at the Old Bailey is £30,000 a day per defendant or £100 a minute, largely a result of the huge legal-aid costs paid courtesy of the taxpayer. Yet the taxpayer's reception in court is neither welcoming nor encouraging. Instead, any effort made by court staff is to *discourage* the public both from seeing justice done and sharing their experience with others. This is not how it is supposed to be in a democracy. As Lord Steyn, chairman of the human rights group JUSTICE and former Lord of Appeal, has put it:

> A criminal trial is a public event. The principle of open justice puts, as has often been said, the judge and all who participate in the trial under intense scrutiny. The glare of contemporaneous publicity ensures that trials

are properly conducted. It is a valuable check on the criminal process. Moreover, the public interest may be as much involved in the circumstances of a remarkable acquittal as in a surprising conviction. Informed public debate is necessary about all such matters. Full contemporaneous reporting of criminal trials in progress promotes public confidence in the administration of justice. It promotes the value of the rule of law.

Reporting the courts

You probably have better things to do than hang around the courts as I've just been doing. But that doesn't mean you don't have a right to know what's happening inside courts or that the cases decided will not have some impact on your life either now or in the future. For those with busy lives, journalists are the means by which the public finds out what happens, so my next port of call is to the main news agencies covering the biggest courts.

Guy Toynes and Scott Wilford are the directors of Central News, an agency of ten reporters covering London's criminal courts and tribunals such as the General Medical Council, Nursing & Midwifery Council, Employment Tribunals and Solicitors Regulation Authority. The agency has existed for twenty-five years and Guy and Scott have been the directors for ten. They know as much about reporting the courts as anyone so I asked them: do you feel able to tell the public the full story about what's happening in court today?

Guy: 'Generally yes, but the court staff need to be told

that the press are not their enemies, rather an essential part of the courtroom process.' He's keen to stress that in the Old Bailey the staff are 'very nice. But in the outer courts it can be so difficult to get the basic info that we're entitled to. One of the fundamental problems is dealing with civil servants [running the courts] who are not aware of what we [and by default the public] are entitled to and when it's asked for we're treated with suspicion.

'We often ask for addresses but the clerk is too busy or they say it's not on file. The address of the defendant is crucial. If we don't have it and there's more than one person with that name (which there usually is) then the copy we write is libellous. We also can't tell the local papers because no one knows where the defendant comes from.

'We started to cover Croydon Crown Court but the court manager flatly refused to give us *any* addresses whatsoever and in the end it was such a hassle that we stopped covering that court. So now Croydon is one of those black holes where who knows what's going on there.'

There is a local newspaper in Croydon but nationwide the press is currently undergoing a massive reorganisation with equally massive redundancies, and most outlets no longer have the time or resources to have these constant running arguments with officials just to get information to which they are legally entitled, let alone do any digging or ask for things outside the norm.

'People do not understand that if the press aren't here there's no point in having a trial in the first place,' Guy says, echoing Lord Steyn. 'If you try and explain this to court staff or barristers they think you're mad. They cannot see the importance of the principle that justice must be seen to be done.'

Guy and Scott work in the windowless basement hovel that is the Old Bailey's press room. It's like going through a time warp to some 1930s Chicago den where the hacks are busily running from one murder trial to the next. The floor is green linoleum, the desks are so old that drawers are missing, and an ancient Hewlett-Packard computer from the 1980s sits abandoned above a rusting filing cabinet. Newspaper clippings decorate yellowed walls and there's the constant hum from some clapped-out ventilation system. Wires hang from various holes in the ceiling. Guy's monitor is propped up by old appointment diaries, his desk ringed with wine and tea stains. Despite all this grub-street chic the two men are dressed in suit and tie.

It doesn't seem entirely a coincidence that the newer the court the less provision given for public and press access. Whereas the original Old Bailey gave ample space for both, Blackfriars and the magistrates courts in Jersey don't even have a press box and public space is at a premium. If you ask the Courts Service or the Ministry of Justice, they'll say all new courtrooms should include provision for reporters, but in practice this space is almost invariably annexed by probation staff, police or court staff – they even put notices on the seats reserving them for themselves, with the result that reporters are left to sit in the public seats. None of the courtrooms in the new Supreme Court have any specific provision for the press nor are there even seats with a desktop on which someone might rest a notebook. Reporters tell of cases where they've been told by security staff to cover a case from the public gallery and although this is contrary to Court Service guidance to staff, most of the security officers in courts are often contracted out from private companies and have no clue about reporters' rights to attend court. Security staff have also demanded that journalists identify themselves and sign in with their names and addresses before admission (often the same courts that withhold the addresses of the defendants oddly enough). There is no justification for this but when your rights to see justice being done are so murky, the only solution is to contact the court manager and how many court watchers are brave enough to do that?

What's also noticeable is that patronage is yet again the order of the day: who you know and how much they like you is the determining factor on whether they'll do you the 'favour' of disseminating so-called 'public information'.

'If you turn up at a Crown court that you've never been to before, the chances of you getting the info to which you're entitled is about zero,' Guy says. This is especially troubling when you consider that most media no longer have full-time court reporters.

As an example of why expert court reporters like those at Central News are needed, let's look at a case for the following day's hearing listed only as 'JGB'. What can anyone make of that? Luckily Scott Wilford knows this involves a US air marshal accused of the rape of a Royal Navy wren during a posting in the UK, but because of the defendant's high position Judge Pontius has granted him anonymity. If we lose reporters like Guy and Scott then this case, like so many others, will be hidden from public view. There used to be twenty-five reporters covering the law courts for Britain's national news bureau the Press Association. By November 2009 there were only four, and such decimation of court reporters is replicated in every news organisation across the UK.

Fortunately some in the judiciary agree that the system must be open in more than name only. The Lord Chief Justice Igor Judge told the Society of Editors conference in November 2009 that the absence of reporters in courts was a major problem for the practice of open justice. 'I'm not comfortable with the thought that you can emblazon open court on the screen if there's no reporter going to walk into the court to observe and then to write up and, where criticism is appropriate, to suggest that it should be made. If there's nobody to walk in, the public interest is damaged. That's the harsh reality.'

He acknowledged that newspapers were facing a battle for survival, beyond the effects of the recession, and also hinted at using technology to make the courts accessible to the people. But we are a long way from that happening, and Lord Judge is rare. Others in the legal profession seem perfectly pleased with the demise of the press and public in court, forgetting entirely that secret justice is no justice at all. Unnecessary obstacles abound – the listing of court cases, for example, is needlessly obscure, giving only the names of parties (and often not even that, as with the new Supreme Court where many cases are listed by letter only: A vs B). Or take another example where a telephone conversation may be used as crucial evidence at a criminal trial yet it is barely audible and so the jury are supplied with a transcript. The press are *sometimes* given a copy of this transcript but never the public.

'I had a stand-up row with a barrister once because the press were refused a copy of such a transcript,' Guy Toynes recalls. 'They had loads of copies but were not making any available to us. It's ludicrous really. If you know the prosecution or defence counsel personally it very often comes down to that.'

Such are the examples by which we know the courts are a system based on patronage. In a democracy everyone should have equal rights to public information and shouldn't need to beg favour or know the right people to see and report justice being done.

The mass of written documents used in a trial is known as 'the bundle'. While barristers and QCs may spend their time perusing and referring to these bundles, they are not actually considered 'public documents' (only the parts referred to in open court are considered 'public'), which leads to a lot of problems reporting the courts accurately and in any meaningful way. When he was Director of Public Prosecutions, Ken Macdonald QC introduced a protocol to end the secrecy shrouding evidence used in open court. The policy, agreed to by the Crown Prosecution Service, the Association for Chief Police Officers and the Society of Editors, guarantees a presumption of disclosure for prosecution material used in court. 'We are determined to provide an open and accountable prosecution process,' Macdonald said in 2005, 'by ensuring that, wherever possible, we give the media access to all relevant prosecution material.'

But when I ask Scott Wilford about accessing the bundles, he just shrugs. 'The protocol might be there but we've seen no evidence of it. No one seems to know who has the authority to release it [the bundle info]. They'll all have to run around and have agreement with themselves. And if anyone baulks then we don't get it. No one seems to know who is in charge.'

A Sketchy Argument

Before we go any further, a brief interlude, in which I ask you to consider the following doodles:

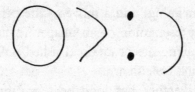

You'll see I'm no artist so it's probably a good thing I've stuck with writing as a profession; I've drawn these two rows of images to see if you can spot something. This is important, so pay close attention.

The two rows feature identical shapes. But whereas in the top row these shapes are broken down individually, in the bottom row they are made into one image. Why is that important? It transpires that if you were to doodle the first row in court you'd be OK, but drawing the bottom doodle could get you done for contempt of court.

I'll try to explain. The top images are not just shapes but writing – shorthand, to be specific. However, put them all together and you get a graphical representation of a face and, in an English court and some Scottish ones too, that's *baaad*. *Verboten*. If you draw this inside a courtroom you'll be chucked out, hectored, scolded, lectured, possibly fined or threatened with jail.

But where precisely do the courts draw the line (small pun intended) between a move of the pen that indicates the symbolic representation of a word (already a semiotic representation of meaning) and a move of the pen that creates a graphical representation of an image? To find out more about this bizarre state of affairs, I asked renowned court sketcher Priscilla Coleman.

The court sketcher has long been a valuable, indeed essential, component in the exercise of justice. A case only becomes real when you know something about the individuals involved. A faceless, nameless victim – even one suffering the most outrageous injustice – will not register with the public. It's how we, as humans, are wired. We need individuality, ideally visual images, to make someone real in our minds. Otherwise it is hard to care, and we should care because the cases that are decided in court go to the very heart of humanity. Take, for example, a case of child abuse – sadly a too common occurrence. Child abuse which leads to murder is less common but not unknown. We want those who commit such appalling crimes brought to justice and we have an overall public interest in ensuring that public services designed to protect endangered children work. In the case of Baby P these services failed catastrophically but it wasn't until the public *saw* Baby P that interest in the case, and demand for reform, developed. Suddenly the faceless victim was a real little boy. However, Coleman was never allowed to sketch the faces of Baby P's killers.

Like the press and public, sketchers have the right to attend open hearings unless the judge makes a specific order of closure. But while reporters can take notes contemporaneously (unless there is a reporting restriction), sketchers must memorise the details of the scene and then *leave the courtroom* to sketch. The reason for this is section 41 of the Criminal Justice Act 1925, which states that no person 'shall take or attempt to take in any court any photograph, or with a view to publication make or attempt to make in any court any portrait or sketch, of any person being a judge of a court or a juror or a witness in or a party to any proceedings before the court, whether civil or criminal'.

When this bill was passed it seems to have done so with little debate. At the second reading of it, the Home Secretary gave the sweeping justification for this sudden restriction of the justice system thus: 'There is a small clause to prevent photographs of the parties being taken in court. Everybody has suffered for a long time by prisoners in the dock and witnesses being pilloried by having their photographs taken, and this is to prevent that happening.'

Yet he was not able to cite a single incident in his speech, even though photography had been around since the middle of the previous century. Photographs had previously been taken of trials to no detrimental effect and a citizen of the 1910s actually had better access to justice than we do today in our great age of democratising technology. Public access was restricted not for any empirical reason or actual proven harm but rather speculated harm, a superstitious belief that public access was inherently bad. Is this not precisely why we criticise theocratic regimes, because their laws are based not on proven facts but on unproven fictions?[3]

Priscilla and I meet in a bar near the Old Bailey. She arrives at our interview carrying a large zippered portfolio in which she carries her sketches and oil pastels. She's from Houston, Texas, and I'm suddenly nostalgic listening to her Southern accent, having had one myself when I worked in South Carolina. She's in her forties and has been sketching trials since she left art school, first in Texas and then in the UK after she moved here in the late eighties to be with her English husband. I ask her exactly what is prohibited.

'There isn't a definitive list,' she tells me.

'Then how do you know what's allowed and what's not?'

Trial and error, it seems – Priscilla learned the hard way how the principle of open justice is interpreted in English courts.

'When I started at ITN they told me you can do little drawings on your notepad but not full sketches. So I was in Jeffrey Archer's libel case. I was drawing little faces of the people in court to go out and have something to refer to.

3. Incidentally it is precisely this superstition which strips jurors of their freedom of speech after a trial. No studies or evidence have ever been done in England showing this endangers justice yet the ban is rigorously enforced. In May 2009 *The Times* was fined £15,000 and Michael Seckerson, the jury foreman, who provided the information to *The Times*, fined £500 for daring to speak out about problems the jury encountered during a trial.

These were tiny, brief sketches.' She draws on her notepad a perfunctory circle with eyes (not all that different from my dazzling efforts above).

'Someone in the public gallery saw my notepad and the faces. They told a court official who came downstairs and around the back and pulled me out of the courtroom. This woman [the court official] was really angry. "What are you doing? Do you realise this is contempt of court? Don't you realise you're not allowed to do a drawing?" I just had to apologise. I thought it was OK just to do a tiny face. I could have been fined as well. £400. Fortunately the woman did let me go back into the court but she took my paper with the faces on it.'

I ask you, ladies and gentlemen of the jury – is this really what we're paying court staff to do? How could this jobsworth know with any confidence that what Priscilla was doing was a contempt of court, since it could have been another variety of shorthand? In fact, that is exactly what those 'faces' were.

Priscilla has since gone on to cover the biggest trials of the last few decades: Baby P's killers and those of Damilola Taylor, the trials of Ian Huntley and Maxine Carr, Rose West, Harold Shipman, Barry George, the Lockerbie bomber Abdelbaset al-Megrahi and Gary Glitter. The Old Bailey and Royal Courts of Justice offer the best facilities – there are press rooms and spaces to work. But if she has to travel to other courts it gets worse.

'There are some court officials who don't know the law. Some of the courts aren't used to having much press attention and then suddenly they're swarmed over with press. They'll let me draw but not always.'

She recalls the trial for the murder of Liverpudlian boy Rhys Jones.

'The court official there was so paranoid he picked me out and had a policeman take me outside and keep me out there. Eventually he allowed me back in but he said: "You can't draw me or the prosecutors" [which is not the law]. He was so worried about me doing something wrong that he didn't want me to do anything.'

Priscilla must sketch outside the court or court precinct, and can draw a picture in as little as fifteen minutes, though prefers to spend at least an hour. She needs somewhere to set up her paper and then gets busy with her oil pastels, but often there is simply nowhere for her to go ('I've worked in ladies' loos before'). If she has to cover a trial at Belmarsh then she's often reduced to sketching in the car park as they close the entire building to public access after the hearing.

Recording the courts

In the age of real-time, zero-cost distribution, the obvious solution to the demise of the court reporter and the plight of the court sketcher is to use modern technology to allow people to see or at least hear trials as they happen or retrospectively. Yet the use of technology for broadcasting justice is firmly resisted by the courts, making it more difficult than ever to see justice being done – or, indeed, heard. It is in the production of transcripts that the greatest injustice is occurring, and there is no clearer example of how justice in Britain is solely for the rich.

Simply put, the courts' refusal to allow people to tape-record open-court proceedings provides an opportunity for a few private companies to monopolise the transcription market. If you want to know what was said in court you have to pay one of these private companies a *lot* of money. It normally costs around £150–250 per hour of court time, and – get this – before the transcription process begins, the courts make you sign a form stating that you will pay *whatever* amount the company decides! If they say it took them fifteen hours to type up the transcript you're obliged to pay 15 x £250 = £3,750. If they say fifty hours that's £12,500. And there's no way to know beforehand how many hours they will charge you for.[4]

'You have to trust them and agree to pay them any amount of money they decide,' Bronagh Taylor told me. She used to be a legal secretary but now works as a researcher at the BBC. 'If there are difficult names and they have to rewind the tape that costs you more. You could be out thousands and thousands of pounds by the time they're done. There's no way round it and there's no way of proving it didn't take the amount of time they tell you. You've nothing to stand on once you've signed that form.'

It's understandable that the typists themselves won't know how long it will take them to transcribe the recordings until they actually begin, but why can't the public make their own recordings or at least have access to any official ones, which they have paid for through their taxes? Many trials in the upper courts are now officially recorded (and in the case of

4. Even the judgments in all criminal, civil, admin and Court of Appeal cases are transcribed by a private company, Merrill Legal Solutions, which has a monopoly. Some judgments are now freely available online at http://www.bailii.org but by no means all.

the new UK Supreme Court, filmed[5]) yet these records are not made available to the public.[6] All High Court hearings began to be digitally recorded from February 2010, but when I spoke to the court's governance officer he told me there were no plans to let the public access these recordings directly. The reason given is one that should be familiar to you by now: unlike private companies, the public can't be trusted, and might change the record so it would no longer be accurate.

As it is, only the rich can afford to have transcripts made, either from the official sound recording or by paying for a court-approved private stenographer. Thus transcripts are the preserve of the wealthy and they remain locked in lawyers' offices never to benefit the general public who are paying for the rest of the judicial system. This, it seems, is the judiciary's idea of open justice – where the vast majority of court proceedings are seen only by a handful of lawyers and court

5. The Supreme Court comes equipped with four cameras in each room and proceedings are routinely filmed but very little of this footage has been broadcast. The only material seen in the court's first few months was the first hearing, in particular a 38-minute clip on US public service channel C-Span and some film from the opening ceremony on 16 October 2009. We can see how important the televising of Parliament has become to public understanding; why can't that be extended to the courts?

6. Another example of the ridiculousness of this prohibition was in 1999 when the hearing for General Pinochet's application for extradition was so packed at Bow Street Magistrates' Court that a closed-circuit TV was set up to accommodate the overflow of reporters. Technically this was a contempt of court but the judges decided that if two conditions were met it was legal: the footage could neither be recorded nor shown outside the court precinct. How's that for showing the public justice being done?

officials while the public pay the bill but see, and hear, nothing.

Section 9 of the Contempt of Court Act 1981 makes it a contempt to use a tape recorder in court without the prior permission of the court. It is also a crime to publish 'a recording of legal proceedings' made in such a way 'by playing it in the hearing of the public or any section of the public'. Current thinking in the judiciary is still in line with the 1974 report by the Phillimore Committee on Contempt of Court which thought that tape recorders 'produce a more dramatic but not necessarily more accurate record of what occurred in court'.

To this 36-year-old argument I counter: what could be more accurate than a verbatim sound recording? Why is it that the police must tape-record interviews with suspects with twin tapes, one of which must be given to the suspect? The reason is because this is considered the most accurate way of recording a proceeding. If this is good enough for the police then why not for the courts?

Court officials say the public might tamper with the tape or mistranslate words in a transcription. Both these problems are just as likely to afflict a private transcriber or indeed a judge. Currently transcripts of cases can be made only with the consent of the presiding judge, who has the right to amend the wording of the judgment (and often does). Some litigants argue they have suffered as a result, with a judge amending what he actually said at the hearing to what he would have liked to have said.

If the concern is with the authenticity of the tape it is very easy to validate a digital file using cryptographic hash functions. And what better way to ensure accuracy of a transcription than to let as many ears as possible hear the oral recording? When there is only one copy of a tape listened to by only one person, accuracy is much lower than if many copies are listened to by many people. So if accuracy is the argument then allow people to record open-court proceedings and post them online. I have a sneaking suspicion, however, that might actually be what puts off the court officials. Could it be they don't want the public seeing what goes on in court?

While most court hearings are at least recorded, tribunals generally are not. When I attended the Information Tribunal hearing for my own case about MPs' expenses in February 2008, I put my tape recorder on the table ready to record every second of this scintillating event for those unable to make it to this open hearing. I was told that I could not record. Everyone seemed to accept this, but to me it seemed like another one of those 'emperor's new clothes' moments. I asked why and was told it just wasn't done. I pressed further and an official said it would be a contempt of court. I let it go at that and took copious notes. But later I regretted that I'd not pushed for a better answer because this hearing became the basis for many articles I wrote and indeed a pivotal scene in the BBC4 dramatisation.[7]

Can we have some rationality here: why else do we pay for such public hearings if not so the public can be informed in the most accurate and comprehensive way about them? Instead, the only public record of this public hearing comes from my and another reporter's notes. How can this be more

7. As a reminder of how rich you have to be to afford transcripts – the BBC budget couldn't stretch to forking out for the transcript of my one-day High Court hearing so instead those scenes had to rely on my notes.

accurate than a verbatim recording? Clearly it's not and yet this is the reality of the current law. I'm confident in my note-taking but I wasn't making a verbatim account and I was rather preoccupied with being a participant in the case.

Later, I went back to the tribunal officials to ask about the prohibition on recording.

Me: Do you know why members of the public are not allowed to tape-record the session? Where is it written that tape recording is not allowed?

Rachel Dunn (*Information Tribunal team leader*): In reference to your query re why tape recording is not allowed by the public there is nothing specifically written within the rules about the tape recording of hearings only that it is up to the discretion of the Tribunal and the Tribunal Panel chair to consider the conduct of the attendees and what may or may not disrupt the progress of the hearing.

Me: I don't see why this can't be done as the hearing is open to the public. Either something is open to the public or not, and if it is then why can't the public make an aural record of it?

John Angel (*Tribunal chairman*): The position of the Information Tribunal is similar to most courts and tribunals. A tribunal does not usually agree to unofficial tape recordings of proceedings because they have the potential to be changed and not be a true record of the proceedings. If a party or any other person attending the hearing makes a recording without the chairperson's consent this could be a contempt of court. If a party wants a transcript of the proceedings then that party should apply to the chairperson, who may then require that a formal transcript of the proceedings be taken. This is expensive so he/she will normally only make such an arrangement if the parties agree to contribute to the cost. If the parties do not want to go to the expense of a transcript but ask for the proceedings to be taped/recorded the chairperson will usually agree to this provided recording equipment is available in the courtroom. Such equipment is rarely available in the venues used by the Information Tribunal. There may be a nominal charge to cover costs of supplying a copy of the tape. Where a party has not contributed to the cost of a transcript he/she may apply for a copy from the transcript service. As we understand it the service will provide a copy two weeks after the hearing for a cost which they determine but which is significantly less than the cost of providing the transcripts during the hearing.

What is the solution? I can tell you what it is not – privatising this very public service, which would serve only to screw the taxpayer further out of information they have already paid to create. Any solution has to be an open source with public formats; if digital recordings are made they should use a common format such as MP3 or similar so that even if a private company is involved there is no difficulty in passing the material back into the public domain. But ultimately I see no good reason why the people should not be allowed to record open-court proceedings themselves and at the very least access official recordings directly.

It's who you know

Let's take a trip down Fleet Street to the Gothic and orna-
mental Royal Courts of Justice also known as the High Court.
I've examined access to criminal courts and now I'm here
to see what access to justice is like in the civil courts. On
any day of the week there are important public issues being
fought here – not just over private contracts but about
medical negligence, judicial reviews of government policy,
life-shattering decisions made in the family courts that have
societal implications, and issues about press freedom and
privacy. The Royal Court is a national court and as such an
arm of government.

It's certainly easier to get inside the building for starters
and the public are right in the courtroom, bums warmed
on wooden benches laid out like church pews in front of
the judge's altar. You get a very intimate experience of justice
in the High Court and I can't recommend it enough. The
cases may not seem as dramatic, but privacy and libel cases
are often noteworthy (and, frankly, entertaining – I once
managed to catch the proprietor of *Express* newspapers
Richard Desmond being quizzed by a QC on his knowledge
of dildos).[8] On the score of seeing justice being done in
person the Royal Courts gets a definite thumbs up, but again
no recording is allowed.

To find out more I asked James Brewster, the editor of
Strand News, an agency of seven reporters covering the Royal
Courts. His office is across the street from the court up a

8. This was Richard Desmond's libel litigation against the biographer
Tom Bower which Desmond lost on 23 July 2009.

tiny spiral staircase that winds past a beauty parlour and a jeweller's. It's another hovel with newspaper clippings on the wall, chipped mugs on chipped lino desks. It's proper old school and I love it. I feel like I'm on the set of *The Front Page*. James is full of energy just like the Central News reporters and I catch him in between covering a case and writing it up. I ask him how well he feels he can tell the public about what is going on in the Royal Courts. He tells me there are two main problems: reporting restrictions and access to documents.

Reporting restrictions are orders made by a judge to prevent a reporter making public what he hears in court. James says his reporters live in fear of making a mistake because there is nothing mandating the order be served on them or even written down.

'You need to be very, very alert. The barrister will just stand up and say "Please can I have this reporting restriction?" and then the judge will say "yes" and if you're not there you won't know about it. We're not served with the order. Occasionally it's put on the door . . . Once we named somebody we shouldn't have. The reporter popped to the loo. A reporting restriction was made. Nobody told us about it. Nothing was served on us and yet technically we could've been done for contempt of court. Fined, sent to prison.'

The bad news is these reporting restrictions are increasing. Ironically, it is the younger judges who are keener on closing courtrooms. Another problem is that many judges make reporting restrictions incorrectly because they rely on what they are told by counsel rather than checking the law themselves.

'In the Court of Appeal there is all due process, full

consideration before imposing a reporting restriction, but in the High Court the judges have grown up with the Human Rights Act. Article 8 [privacy] has led to a change in the atmosphere of court to the point where the basic principle that there should be public access that is only prevented for exceptional reasons is now such that those reasons need not be exceptional.'

A new fetishisation of privacy has taken hold and cases, particularly involving medical negligence or children, which used to be reported as a matter of course are now closed. We can see what sort of negative societal effect such closed justice has by looking at the myriad problems that have erupted as a result of closure of the family courts. Some social services departments and experts are consistently seeing abuse, especially 'emotional harm', where there is none, and in other instances local authorities have flagrantly ignored the legal requirement that there should be minimum intervention in family life. Yet none of these issues can be addressed unless the courts are opened up. Social workers, judges and expert witnesses – all of whom are often vital to proceedings – can't be held accountable.[9] In addition, the High Court regularly issues injunctions prohibiting publication of various things but there is no central record of such orders so a request for a copy of any particular order

9. Camilla Cavendish has written extensively about the problems of secret family courts in her columns for *The Times*, and argues that it 'should be perfectly possible to keep children's and parents' names out of the press while reporting the evidence in full [since] the media does this routinely in rape cases. But in the family division, reporting restrictions are enshrined in ten statutes, some of which can only be changed by Parliament.'

will be met by blank stares unless you know the case number and, more likely, the name of the issuing judge and the date the order was issued. Many of these orders are open-ended, so you could easily be found in contempt for having breached an order which was made years earlier but which you had no way of knowing even existed.

These are some of the problems with proceedings. What about documents?

'In court there's a big gap between what we're theoretically allowed to see and what we actually get to see,' James says. 'We're allowed to see claim forms and particulars [in the hearing]. We get them from the court clerk in the courtroom but nine times out of ten those documents haven't actually made it to the court file so we don't get access to them. For some reason they get stuck in the office bureaucracy so when we ask can we see the papers they say: "No, terribly sorry, we haven't got them."'

Inevitably, it comes down to that great British tradition of knowing the right people and keeping them sweet.

The evidence from the bundles mentioned in open court is a public record, but again there is nothing requiring a copy to be made available to the public. The clerks don't often have copies and so anyone wanting to see these records is entirely dependent on the whim of the parties' lawyers. If they refuse access then you have to make an application to the judge.

'It's wrong that independent reporters should be beholden to the parties and their lawyers in this way to access public documents,' James says. 'It gives them the opportunity, which they sometimes use, to exclude the press without any judicial intervention. And it makes us feel like a PR agency because we're put into a position where we could be used by the parties' lawyers to get their message across.'

Bronagh Taylor agrees. 'If you know people then it's easier.' She says even lawyers can find it difficult to get documents from court. 'It can often depend on the law firm – if you're a prestigious one then you get things a lot easier. I've had other solicitors call me and say: "Can you try and get this because I've tried and I can't get it?" It is definitely who you know and who you work for.'

Technically, 'originating process' documents – that is, all writs and claim forms – are public, but the reality is that they provide very little meaningful information. You're given a writ book simply showing all the claim forms that have been issued but no factual detail, just *Bloggs* vs *Bloggs*. If you want to search for a specific case then you have to pay a search fee. The sorts of investigations we did in America using court records to discern patterns of malpractice, abuse or litigious bullying by companies or institutions simply cannot be done in England and people are left to be defrauded, abused and put in danger as a result.

As James Brewster sums it up: 'You can't have a democratic society without covering one of the arms of government.' But he knows all too well that as newspapers are cutting budgets so his own budget is cut to the wire and court reporting is not what it was or should be. The difficulty accessing documents only makes it more expensive and time consuming.

Can it be this bad? I decide to try and get my hands on some court documentation. I used to do this in America when I was covering for the court reporter. I would trundle along to the clerks office, say 'hi' and introduce myself as the covering court reporter, and then spend the next thirty to sixty minutes going through all the court filings. If I wanted more details from a case I'd ask the clerk, who would pull the file, and I'd make photocopies. This all took a minimum of fuss and effort and was at no cost and very little inconvenience to the staff. I simply did my own thing and they let me. That was a county court but it's the same in pretty much any American court. At the US Supreme Court you can find all this online, same with Australia, Canada, New Zealand and South Africa. Now let's see the English equivalent.

I head to the East Block of the High Court to a section bizarely called 'the bear garden' where cases are filed. I'm going to use Jane Clift's case against Slough Borough Council, which I talk about in the next chapter, as my test case. I have the names of the parties (which is more than most people will have) but when I talk to the clerk in the customer information office he says I need the case number. Without it, no deal.

'How do I get that?' I ask naively. 'Is there a database somewhere I can look it up?'

To get the case number I have to go to the search room. along the hall. Here I have a friendly chat with a man who says that in order to search I must pay a fee of £5 per fifteen minutes of searching. But I have to pay the fee before I search. 'How will I know how long it will take to find something before I start searching?' He says he'll be lenient with me. 'I'm not going to hassle you every five minutes, but if there's a queue then you'll have to go back and pay more money, though if you have the names then fifteen minutes should be enough.'

I head to the fees office, which is inconveniently placed at the other end of the corridor and round a corner. There is another queue. Here you wait and then pay your fee. Armed with this receipt I head back to the search room where hopefully I'll get my case number. Then armed with this it's back to the customer information room where I fill out a form requesting the documents I want. Then it's another wait, from two to five days. If you want a photocopy then it's another trip over to the fees office. You'll pay £5 for the first ten pages, and 50p per page for subsequent pages. These charges apply to each document individually. If I wanted to see anything from the case files (which I do) then I would need permission for which I would have to complete another form and pay another fee (currently £75 if the application is on notice and £40 if the application is without notice or by consent). I'd have to go before a 'master' to explain why, in the interests of justice, I should be given access. Surely in a democracy the default position should be the opposite: the case open unless someone explains to the 'master' why it needs to be sealed. Fortunately I can forgo these last stages because I happen to know the law firm that represented Jane Clift as they represented me against the House of Commons (remember, it's all about who you know).

That's four different people in four parts of the East Block just to get one document which exists most likely in electronic form and could have been given to me at no cost whatsoever and without inconveniencing four different people.

The entire justification given by the government for imposing fees is to cover administrative costs, but these costs are entirely artificial. Records can be filed electronically and as such the cost of duplication is zero. The court is making needless work for itself.

James Brewster isn't asking for a lot to cover the courts effectively. 'I would like to see the courts living up to what the rules actually say. So that in practice we do get access automatically to the documents we are allowed to see.'

The list of documents automatically and readily available should be:

1. claim form
2. particulars of claim
3. skeleton arguments (where the parties lay out their argument)
4. witness statements once admitted into evidence[10]

'If we just had those four we could cover every case. But you'd be amazed how difficult it is to get simply the minimum.'

I could go on:

- Public access to case law is only for the rich through private legal databases; even access to the raw data needed to create a statute law database is continually blocked by officials at the Ministry of Justice despite over £1 million of public money being spent on the project.
- The new Supreme Court, which was meant to be a

10. Other courts such as the Canadian Supreme Court and US Supreme Court provide all this information and more to the public online at no cost.

model of a new age of open justice, charges the public a minimum of £350 a time to access documents.

- A number of trials are now held in private using secret evidence not available even to the defendant.[11]
- A children, schools and families bill makes it a contempt of court to report all but a tiny fraction of family court proceedings no matter the public implications.

All manner of good reasons may be put forward for such secrecy, but once the right of the people to see justice being done is eroded, it is not long before there is no justice at all.

We have a justice system paid for by the common people but whose proceedings are available only to the few: the legal profession and the rich, powerful or privileged.

Where reporters were once a substitute for the people's inability to go to the courts in person, now the media are under threat and what little resources remain are spent battling to gain access to information that should be automatically in the public domain. I came across the state's silence even while writing this chapter. In August 2009 I put in my first interview request to the director of the Royal Courts of Justice. I was told he could not talk to me and I was referred instead to the Ministry of Justice press office. After repeated promises to get back to me with answers or

11. A report on secret evidence by the legal human rights organisation JUSTICE in June 2009 revealed how in the last twelve years, the British traditions of open justice and the right to a fair hearing have been undermined by the use of secret evidence in closed hearings.

even an interview, four months passed and I received no information at all from the ministry.

The courts are in danger of becoming an elitist enclave entirely separate and out of touch with modern society. The privatisation of court transcripts and the numerous restrictions on the public seeing justice done – from the prohibition on sketching and recording to the poorly resourced public galleries – all betray an attitude that the information from open courts doesn't belong to the public but to lawyers and court officials. The justice system is becoming a closed world, a cloistered sanctum of the legal profession, for which we pay the bill.

We pay a lot of money for our judicial system[12] though not enough. An open system with a jury costs more than a secret system with only a judge. In the past this cost was considered one worth bearing for the long-term health of our democracy. Increasingly, though, politicians have not thought it worthwhile to bear these costs. Fewer trials have juries and fewer members of the public are able to see justice being done. Less is spent on the courts and money that could be used to improve the judicial system is instead diverted to reactionary policing methods and universal surveillance for which there is no evidence of effectiveness.

Let's turn now to the first step in the criminal justice system – the police.

---

12. The initial set-up costs of the new Supreme Court for which the public have paid but cannot see in action was £56.9 million.

7

Crime and Punishment

The police are the physical force backing up the state's power. They are also our first port of call when things go wrong or we need protection. It is precisely because the police have a monopoly on legitimate force that we need to make sure they work *for* us, not against us.

The best way to do this is to ensure the police answer directly to the community they are policing. This is what the original principles set out by Robert Peel in 1829 were all about. When Peel created the first organised police force in London (the Metropolitan Police), the British public were highly sceptical about granting such powers to an arm of the state. Peel put forward a list of nine simple principles to which the police had to adhere if they were to enjoy public trust, and trust is essential for effective policing:

Police, at all times, should maintain a relationship with the public that gives reality to the historic tradition that the police are the public and the public are the police;

the police being only members of the public who are paid to give full-time attention to duties which are incumbent upon every citizen in the interests of community welfare and existence.

This fundamental understanding between the police and the public, so crucial in Peel's day, has now been lost. The modern-day version would instead read: *the police are the politicians and the politicians are the police*, with the public left out of the loop entirely. I could cite numerous examples of this but for the sake of brevity I'm going to focus in this chapter on one of the most alarming trends in twenty-first-century policing, whereby those who challenge the state's definition of crime and punishment become marginalised, even criminalised. Remember Philip Balmforth, the West Yorkshire police officer from Chapter 2? He's only one of scores of officers punished for daring to put the public first. Philip was stripped of his national public role on forced marriage, but he was at least allowed to continue working in the force. Another police officer who dared to question one force's use of covert surveillance was himself put under surveillance and his friend (who happened to be a journalist) was arrested and threatened with life in prison.

Bugging you – the story of Mark Kearney and Sally Murrer

I'm watching one of the watchers who sits across from me in a pub near Euston Station. Mark Kearney is with his friend and former partner Sally Murrer. Mark is a retired copper; to be precise he was once a Thames Valley police detective, a covert surveillance and intelligence officer. His eyes are soft blue with long dark lashes in a tanned face highlighted by white hair. He's in his fifties, still in good shape, and looks like someone you'd want on your side if a fight broke out. Sally Murrer is the same age, petite with dark brown ringleted hair and large chestnut eyes. She has an open, questing face and while we talk she sucks on a plastic cigarette, as she's been trying to give up smoking for years. Their personal history is complicated; they are both married to other people and have three children each. They're clearly very close.

It was this closeness which got them into trouble in the spring of 2007. They had met fifteen years earlier when Mark was the press officer at Thames Valley Police and Sally was a part-time reporter on the *Milton Keynes Citizen*, where she still works. Mark left Thames Valley to join the Regional Crime Squad then later the National Crime Squad, returning to Thames Valley in 2000. He and Sally rekindled their friendship (Sally was by then married) and became lovers in 2001. Today they remain best friends, seeing each other so regularly that their two families with six kids are almost intermingled.

You might think the police have better things to worry about than a copper's ex-girlfriend – like responding to crime – but apparently not. What seemed to disturb the authorities in particular was Sally's profession. There is nothing unusual about cops and reporters hanging out together. In the old days of crime reporting this was commonplace and it was not unduly difficult to strike a balance between keeping the public informed without endangering investigations. But in the age of PR and spin, such free conversations are looked upon by the authorities with great suspicion. They are considered highly dangerous – not to policing (after all, reporters and police worked perfectly well together for decades with no ill effects to society) but dangerous to those in power: specifically politicians and the police chiefs. Such free conversations might lead to challenging questions or demand for reform. The authorities were particularly worried because Mark knew things they definitely didn't want the public knowing.

In 2007, Mark was working as part of a secret intelligence unit at Woodhill prison near Milton Keynes which bugged inmates' telephones and their visits. When a supervising officer from a police force wanted someone bugged, they had to go to Mark. Mark didn't have the authority to deny these requests but increasingly he was becoming uncomfortable with their frequency. As a trained surveillance officer he believed such covert bugging should be used sparingly, as a last resort and with some probable cause rather than as a commonplace used lazily to substitute for the harder work of actual investigation. And it wasn't just prisoners being bugged – it was their visitors, too. One of those visitors happened to be an MP, Sadiq Khan.[1] Mark had been

---

1. I love the way MPs couldn't give two hoots about the erosion of our privacy or civil liberties up until the point when their *own* privacy or civil rights are invaded. When MPs discovered that one of their own was being bugged, they had a sudden change of heart about the laws they'd passed granting the police wide-ranging and discretionary surveillance powers. Their outrage didn't extend to the bugging of innocent people, only MPs, who as Right Honourable gentlemen and ladies thought themselves beyond reproach.

instructed to record conversations with Babar Ahmad, a terror suspect, in 2005 and 2006. The bugging was carried out, according to the court record, at the request of the Metropolitan Police, which had been monitoring Ahmad's communications since he was arrested on an American extradition warrant in 2004. Mark said he was also asked by West Midlands Police to listen in when another terrorist inmate was visited by his solicitor, in spite of protections on legal professional confidentiality.

Believing that many of the bugging operations he was being asked to conduct were illegal, unwarranted or unjustified, Mark referred several of them to the prison governor. This did not please some police officers and, perhaps not coincidentally, it was at precisely this time that Mark found *himself* under surveillance.

'I thought he was going mad,' Sally says. 'I told him the strain was getting to him, that he ought to go see a therapist.'

But Mark was right. His car *was* bugged and he *was* under surveillance.

Operation Plaid was a joint investigation by Thames Valley Police's Professional Standards Department and Hertfordshire Police. Were there allegations that Mark was corrupt, untrustworthy or had abused his position in the myriad ways police sometimes do? No. Their suspicions were aroused by what they saw as Mark's dissent, merely his voiced reservations about the bugging operations and his referral to the prison governor of the more questionable orders. For this he was marked out as suspect; his friendship with a journalist only made matters worse. The intent of Operation Plaid was to find out whether information was being passed to journalists and to use the full powers of the police (and then some) to identify journalistic sources.

The operation began in mid-February 2007 and the officers were soon intercepting all Mark and Sally's phone calls and text messages. Mark took a month's leave and arrived back in the country on 27 March. On 30 March the police bugged his car. Four days later, Mark realised he was being followed as well. The surveillance went on until 8 May.

After nearly two months of surveillance the police made their move. Mark was phoned on his way to work one morning and told to report to the police station where he was arrested. Eight police officers were also waiting at Sally's house and another four searched the newspaper office. They took her notebooks, computers, phone and contacts book. She'd moved house just six days earlier, so no one knew her new number. Her eldest daughter was scheduled to take her first GCSE in two days' time and all her coursework was on the home computer, so she had to get an extension to redo it all.

'I was absolutely convinced I would go to prison,' Sally told me. 'The ferocity of the investigation was unbelievable. They won't stop till they get me, I thought. They told me I'd go to prison for life.'

Police accused Sally of obtaining confidential information from Mark and then selling it to the national press. They charged her with three counts of the ancient common-law offence of aiding and abetting misconduct in a public office. Mark's twenty-year-old soldier son was also charged with one count and a private detective and retired police officer Mark knew named Derek Webb, aged fifty-three, of Harpenden, faced five counts. Kearney was charged with eight counts of wilful misconduct in a public office.

Mark recognised the multiple arrests as 'hostage taking' – a common method of intimidation by the police. 'You arrest all those closest to someone in an attempt to make them do what you want.'

What, I ask Mark, did they want him to do?

'They wanted me to keep quiet about what I knew.'

The charges made against Mark, Sally, Derek and Mark's son were thrown out when Judge Southwell ruled the evidence inadmissible in court because the police had not followed proper procedure in relation to a journalist's right to carry out their jobs, but that was eighteen months later. Had the case gone to trial, it would have cost more than £4 million; it still ended up costing in excess of £1 million of public money. What were Thames Valley Police thinking?

'The leaking of sensitive information is a serious matter which can jeopardise police investigations, put officers and members of the public at risk and lead to criminal and misconduct charges,' the force said, invoking as ever the cause of national security. 'The public has a right to expect that officers and police staff who have access to sensitive information can be trusted to handle the material appropriately.'

So who was this Sally Murrer, putting officers and members of the public at risk with her reports in the *Milton Keynes Citizen*, and what was this great threat to national security?

Here's the background on Sally. She's a middle-aged mother with three children now aged twelve, nineteen and twenty-two. Her eldest, James, is severely autistic and until she was arrested Sally worked part-time so she could care for him. After the arrest she had to put him into a residential care home and send her middle child to boarding school. She works twelve hours a week on a paper with a weekly distribution of 100,000 copies and has been a local journalist for thirty years. She's the sort of reporter that all communities used to have but now few do. It's precisely because of her local knowledge that she's such a valuable journalist. But that's also precisely why she was deemed a 'threat' by Thames Valley Police. Sally's ability to speak directly to police officers was looked upon as criminal by this highly politicised police press office.

As Sally told one of the interrogating police officers: 'I was under the impression we'd been batting for the same side and I batted very hard for you guys and I think I now don't trust you enough to go into detail . . . What I can say if Thames Valley Police are genuinely interested in their service to the press over the past six weeks [is that] I've been contacted by dozens of journalists from all over the place who share the same opinion that there are leaks if you call them that – we like to think we're helping and that police officers are enthusiastic and they [the leaks] have come about because the press system is appalling . . . I would love to get back to the old days of a good, healthy, trusted working relationship where we're all concentrating on what we're all pretty good at and that's keeping our streets safe and providing a service.'

The main accusation the police made against Sally was that she knew about a murder victim's past conviction for drugs. They claimed she had gained this 'confidential' information from Mark.

'We saw on the news desk a police report about this murder and the police were making out this guy Douglas

Belcher was a pillar of the community,' Sally told me. 'I recognised the name immediately. His wife Veronica Belcher is secretary to Phyllis Starkey, our Labour MP for Milton Keynes. I remembered that this Belcher had something dodgy about him, that he'd been to prison, but I couldn't remember why. Mark and I were talking about that. "Do you remember that story I wrote?" I asked Mark when I saw him. Mark said, "I'm sure it was drugs." So I looked back in the files and found the story and it was for drugs.'

Sally read her old story and found that far from being a model citizen Belcher had spent ten years in a French prison for drugs smuggling. She still had the telephone number for his lawyer, Stephen Jakobi, and called him for an interview. She passed her notes from the interview to the reporter who was working the story, Rob Hartley, and he asked the police press office for a comment on Belcher's past. The next day the police held a press conference in which they said they'd found a cannabis factory behind a hidden door in Belcher's house.

On the Wednesday following the publication of the story and the police press conference, Sally and Mark were talking about the case in his car. It was this bugged conversation which the police claimed showed evidence of Mark giving Sally confidential information, and which triggered their arrest. Only when Sally's solicitors were given access to the evidence against her did it become clear that everything the police were claiming was 'leaked' (i.e. the details of Belcher's criminal past) was in fact already in the public domain.

'The thing that upset me the most was the bugging of the

phones and texts. To read all that back in black and white was horrible. Mark and I are very, very close. We used to have a relationship and we are still best friends. When we see each other we basically offload all sorts of personal stuff. There were maybe two or three hundred hours of conversations. The stuff they used from all that totalled three to four minutes. The rest of it was really personal stuff. Nothing whatsoever to do with the case at all.'

Another shocker was to come. Reading the official transcript from her police interview which was used as evidence against her, it could appear as though Mark told Sally something confidential. But when Sally's lawyers at Simons Muirhead & Burton got hold of the actual police recording and listened to all the tapes, they discovered large sections of Sally's rebuttals omitted. The police can't alter the time code on tapes so they accounted for the missing sections by saying the tape was inaudible or had a fault.

'Once we got hold of those tapes and played them back we discovered they were perfectly intelligible,' Sally says. 'We half wanted to go to trial. It would have exposed so many things that were wrong with the police . . . How they set out single-mindedly with a story in their heads and then they got permission to bug us (incorrectly in my case) and then they were so determined to get something out of it they tried to tailor the facts to fit – by any means possible [including] deliberately missing out bits of transcript.'

CRIME AND PUNISHMENT

I got hold of these transcripts thanks to Sally's lawyers. In the following excerpt, all text in bold was omitted from the official version, which ran to just under 150 words. 'SAN' refers to Sally, '3354' her interrogator, 'Sol' her solicitor.

SAN	Yeah, definitely. That's how I knew.
3354	**Does he tell you everything about incidents?**
SAN	**No he doesn't.**
3354	A little bit later **down you say . . . the safe in Doug Belcher's house.** How do you know about the safe?
SAN	From the press conference.
3354	**That was mentioned at the press conference?**
SAN	**Yes.**
3354	Mark then says 'it wasn't a safe it was a false wall [inaudible]'. You say 'a false wall'. Did you know it was a false wall prior to the conversation with Mr KEARNEY?
SAN	**No but the reporter who was covering the story did. It had all come out. I wasn't writing the story. I was just gossiping, it wasn't my story.**
3354	**So you were** [unclear] Mark about an ongoing confidential investigation?
SAN	**Yes I was, I was doing that thing again which you say is wrong and I'm really sorry.**
3354	**There's a few more bits and pieces of conversation down that page.** A bit further down at 12:12 Mark says 'they burst in there and they found all these cannabis plants, skunk and all sorts'.
SAN	Yeah, I told him about that.
3354	You told me . . . **he's a huge pillar of the community and he laughs. He's done about 10 years on a drug importation.**

SAN	This is only information that I told him; I wrote about the 10 years sentence.
3354	OK, why is Mark Kearney telling you this information?
Sol	I'm not quite sure, and obviously this is Sally's interview and not mine . . . Sally had written an article about Mr Belcher 10 years previously, so that's why . . .
SAN	You've obviously missed a phone call between us or something where I've said 'Oh . . .'
3354	That has nothing to do with the safe or drugs or [unclear]
SAN	Again, I've just come from the office, and that has come from, I mean I'm sure you can substantiate that with other reporters. So Mark's relaying to me again what I told him, which is what I've said in the Mcleod story, its bizarre yes, it's bizarre I totally agree.
3354	Then at 12.12.20 Mark says 'I told you tie him in with the drugs didn't I' but you said 'no no no it's not a drugs charge'. Explain this.
SAN	Because we were arguing about the story that I'd written previously, and couldn't remember whether it was drugs or not. I knew . . . I spoke around the office, going 'Doug Belcher, Doug Belcher . . . I know the name', France, and because he was an old human rights activist and he was a member of the Communist Party, I was thinking that I'd written about him in some political context because I'd got politics on my brain because of Veronica Belcher, who is secretary to Phyllis Starkey the MP, who's a contact of mine, so I'm [unclear] thinking 'what is it, what is it, what is it' and then suddenly the drugs angle comes up and the police say yes there's this cannabis factory, and I'm thinking 'drugs' and as soon as they said drugs I remembered there's a lawyer called Stephen Jackaby [SIC], and if you . . . it's not on the transcript, but the tape runs on. I thought yes [unclear] Stephen Jackaby, fair trials abroad, he specialises, he set up his own company to defend drug . . . people who are caught with drugs, traditionally in bits of their car, the side of their car, and he's defended a host of these cases. I hadn't spoke to him for years, looked in my contacts book, and you have the book, with

numbers in there, and hopefully you have the notebook because it was when Stephen Jackaby . . . I rang him up [unclear] and said 'it's Sally Murrer from the Citizen' and he said 'yes I remember you, Doug Belcher – 2000/199 . . . whatever, he's got this razor sharp brain. He said yes he was done for drugs and at that point the whole office goes 'drugs, of course', the whole story, the jigsaw if you like, fitted into place.

3354 | So you're talking at this time about the false walls and the plants and the plants that were growing?

SAN | Yes. I'd already made the call to Stephen Jackaby, I'm telling Mark, I'd interviewed Phyllis Starkey for a piece in the paper I didn't write but I wrote a memo to the reporter with Phyllis Starkey's comments, which is on my computer, you'll see it. That was given to the reporter. It's all retrospective, it's all done – he's not given me any information to print. Everything was retrospective. He's talking about things that have already been printed, and made out that he's . . .

3354 | Yeah but he's saying 'I told you to tie him with drugs didn't I'.

SAN | Yeah when we had the conversation . . . as the story was going to press or just before it was printed [unclear] because there were two stories about him. The first one was [unclear] we didn't know what was going on, man out of a van; I don't think I was in that day. He's saying . . . I'm saying 'what is it, what is it, what is it?'

3354 | But he's telling you 'I told you to tie him with drugs didn't I', why did he say that?

SAN | Because we'd already got evidence of the drugs in the house; he's got the drugs everywhere. I'm saying it wasn't drugs it was politics, it's something to do with the Communist Party and Phyllis Starkey, and Mark said it was drugs.

3354 | So he's told you about it before, that it was drugs?

SAN | Yes but nothing was printed.

3354 | This is an ongoing, serious, criminal investigation and he's telling you about it, and he's telling you, he said 'I told you to tie him with drugs didn't I'.

SAN	He hadn't got any concrete information; if he had . . .
3354	'I told you to tie him with drugs didn't I'. How's that not concrete?
SAN	Can you tell me then, if that's the case and he told me that – I assume he was just hypothesising about it – how come the first story the Citizen did, we didn't tie him in with drugs, we were being totally naïve about it. It was Stephen Jackaby that tied him in with the drugs, and I am then relaying information to Mark about what I had found out. I'm giving information to him.
3354	So when did he tell you to tie it to drugs?
SAN	When I said I'd written about him before; he was held in France, and Mark said well that would have been drugs. I said . . .
3354	No, you're not talking . . . you're talking here about the present time, about the search teams and the cannabis and the plants that were growing in the house; that's exactly [unclear] it wasn't a safe, it was a false wall it was a hydroponics [unclear] then it comes 'I told you to tie him into drugs': it's within 9 seconds that you're talking about the cannabis plants and everything growing there and then he said 'I told you to tie him with drugs didn't I'.
SAN	It was obviously a previous conversation, because there was no question of drugs, he didn't say . . .
3354	So why was he telling you?
SAN	I think I'm saying that I've written about this man before; I can't think what the story is. He was arrested in France and held and Mark said that would have been drugs and I said it wasn't drugs, no no no.
3354	Alright, we've exhausted that one, let's change the tape because it's just about to go.

There were two other alleged leaks. One was about a former Milton Keynes Dons footballer arrested after a fight at a party in a busy hotel (in fact the paper had a tip-off from a member of the public, as did the rival *Milton Keynes News*). The other related to a fifteen-year-old boy who was freed from prison despite telling officials he was going to become a suicide bomber. This 'leak' was never published and the first time Sally learned the boy's name was when she read it in the police disclosure of her own case. Neither of these alleged leaks jeopardised national security – indeed, in the latter claim one might argue *not knowing* would have been more dangerous to the public. Let's just remember that Peelian principle – the police are the public and the public are the police. The danger with a centralised police PR operation is that information is used not to benefit the public but to benefit those in power, often to the detriment of the public. It is for this reason that so many front-line officers 'leak', because they want to solve their cases and they know they can only do so with the help and cooperation of the public. A propagandist approach to policing serves only to alienate the public and that makes it harder to solve cases.

Another principle was at stake, too. The right of journalists in a democratic society to do their jobs – i.e. talk to people. That's what reporters do in free countries. They try to figure out what's going on behind the spin. Under Article 10 of the Human Rights Convention, Sally's right to freedom of expression had been breached by the state. Thames Valley Police had no right to bug her conversations with Mark, a confidential source, and her arrest was therefore unlawful and the 'evidence' ruled inadmissible. The stories she wrote were accurate and any information printed was already in the public domain.

The police are no longer working for the people when they use the law to criminalise a key element of democracy: keeping people informed. It is certainly not in the public interest for corruption, embarrassment and outright lawbreaking to be hidden under the guise of 'protecting national security'. Yet this is just one example of the police putting their own political interests over the public interest. Before relating one final story of crime and punishment – one that would be hilarious if it weren't so disturbing – let's look at two types of information that are currently classed as 'confidential': criminal incident data and criminal records.

Crime data – for police eyes only

The best way to gauge the effectiveness of the police is how they respond and deal with crime, and the only way to know this is for criminal incident data to be public. As local reporters continue to lose support, how else are you going to hear about a burglary in your neighbourhood, beyond word of mouth? If there were a string of sexual assaults done at a particular time in a particular park, you would be none the wiser and may very well put yourself at risk by walking through this park at precisely this time. Why should we be kept in ignorance about the crime that is happening around us? We have every right to know.

Remember our man Richard Pope from Chapter 5 who

was threatened by the Royal Mail for his civic activism? Well, he's a man of many ideas and a few years ago he decided to build a civic website using crime data mapped out with a discussion forum where neighbours could talk about problems in their area and liaise with their local police officer. A great idea? The police didn't think so.

'We couldn't get any raw data,' Pope says, 'so the project never got off the ground.'

It seems ludicrous that, sitting in my flat in London, I can look online to see what's happening on a street in Chicago and yet know nothing about what's happening outside my own front door in London. Crime maps such as: www.spotcrime.com and http://chicago.everyblock.com/crime were built not by the police but enterprising citizens because in the US all but a few police forces make their crime data public. I asked the man who runs www.spotcrime.com if he knew of any harm that had resulted from putting this criminal incident data online.

'I don't know of any harm and it's something we discuss here quite a bit,' Colin Drane said. 'There's the obvious argument about property values, but this seems to mean that buyers are not supposed to have access to the same information that sellers have.'

After sustained campaigning on this issue by myself and others, the Metropolitan Police now publishes some data, but it only relates to property crimes, not violent crime, and the data is not particularly timely, is aggregated into large, artificial geographic regions called 'super-output' areas and not at all user-friendly. The Met cites 'privacy' as one reason not to release more detailed crime data, but crimes are not a great secret, particularly not violent crimes,[2] and the technology exists to anonymise data. Richard Pope speculates the main problem may be that police are not technically savvy enough, citing an encounter he had at a meeting between locals, the council and the police where the Met admitted it couldn't provide incident detail broken down by area – so the council ended up paying the Met just to get this information.

This would be hard to believe had we not read all the previous chapters about how anonymity and lack of accountability lead to overall inefficiency. State-mandated ignorance benefits no one.

For crime data to be useful and trustworthy it must be:
- timely – within a week of the incident, not months, or, as is the case with the Home Office, years
- locatable – broken down by street or the first section of a postcode
- detailed – we don't need names and exact addresses but we do need to know the type of crime, when it happened and where

---

2. This bleating on about protecting our privacy is not without some irony as this is the same force that films and keeps extensive files on innocent people who dare dissent by protesting. Police surveillance units, known as Forward Intelligence Teams (FIT) and Evidence Gatherers, video and photograph campaigners as they enter and leave openly advertised public meetings then store this data on force-wide databases so police can chronicle the campaigners' political activities.

The lucrative trade in criminal records

One of the allegations made against Mark and Sally related to Sally's knowledge that Doug Belcher had a previous conviction for drugs. She knew that because she happened to be the reporter who had written the story ten years earlier. Now why should his previous conviction – which was handed down in open court – be a state secret?

Technically, all criminal convictions are public records as they are handed down in open court. However, the reality is inconsistency, confusion and overriding paternalism. True, the records are public, but only if you happen to go to every court hearing in every court in the entire country. If a newspaper reporter happens to cover a trial then that conviction will be in the paper's archives and therefore publicly accessible (like Belcher's). However, as we saw in Chapter 6, the number of court reporters has plummeted so public access via the media is now extremely rare, and it's not as if the courts are bending over backwards to make sentences or court lists publicly available.

There is another, even more bizarre issue. Despite hundreds of millions of pounds of public money spent to gather criminal sentences, in their *collected* form, criminal convictions are top secret. More than that, it is a criminal offence to access them. The private company Capita was given £400 million of public money to build the main criminal records database and received another £68 million in 2004, despite being late and overbudget. Access to this publicly funded database is granted only to the police and registered companies or certain voluntary organisations. All this costs money – lots of it. The Criminal Records

Bureau standard check costs £26 (reduced from £31 in October 2009 after sustained criticism) and an enhanced check is £36. These need to be reapplied for with each new job or after a certain time period, ensuring a continual income flow. Just as we've seen with court transcripts, postcodes, mapping data and parliamentary records, criminal sentences may be public in principle but the prohibition on public access creates a monopoly for an organisation or a private company that can then charge usurious rates – in this case to 'protect' us. The CRB's own website makes no secret about how it courts big business with a sales pitch equating business success with criminal vetting: 'Detecting criminal convictions before job candidates are hired and represent your company is crucial in protecting your business's reputation . . .'

Because people cannot do background checks as their own individual circumstances warrant, the state must constantly increase the number of people undergoing mandatory checks. Even children must be vetted before they can work with other children. A freedom-of-information request to the CRB in December 2009 revealed that since 2002 over 43,000 under-sixteens have had to undergo CRB vetting, 3,000 of whom were actually thirteen or younger. One can't help thinking that the profit motive is the main driver behind the 400 per cent increase in the number of fourteen-year-olds undergoing CRB checks since 2002.

The Association of Chief Police Officers has recently got in on the act, usurping the CRB checks by requiring its own for visas to Australia, Canada, New Zealand, South Africa and the United States of America. ACPO checks run at £35 (standard), £70 (premium), with £5 for each additional copy.

The government is also keen to get a piece of this pie and in 2009 it created the Independent Safeguarding Authority 'to help prevent unsuitable people from working with children and vulnerable adults'. Common sense indicates people are best placed to do this themselves – parents can run checks on those who care for their child, or relatives for carers of a family member. We, however, cannot be trusted. Instead, the ISA breezily promises to 'assess every person who wants to work or volunteer with vulnerable people. Applicants will be assessed using data gathered by the CRB, including relevant criminal convictions, cautions, police intelligence and other appropriate sources.'

This is simply not going to work for all the reasons I laid out in Chapter 4 about the failures of big bureaucracy. There are not enough people to police the system and the cost will be colossal. The taxpayer will be hit twice – firstly to fund the creation of this unwieldy bureaucracy and secondly each time he or she is forced to buy a criminal records check.

So opaque are the vetting regulations that even its own officials can't agree who will and will not fall under its purview. Just like the children's database in Chapter 1, the law on vetting doesn't actually specify who will be covered and what precise data will be captured.

Here are just a few of the ridiculously complex requirements:

- If an individual has a new job starting in September 2010, they will not have to be on the database, but if their job starts in November 2010, they will have to register on the database and if they do not they will be committing a crime, punishable by up to a £5,000 fine.

- If you volunteered once a month in January, February and March, you will have to be registered on the vetting database; but if you volunteered in January, February and April, you do not.
- Sixteen-year-olds have to be registered on the vetting database if they are helping out at a local care home, but not if they are teaching members of their own peer group.
- If an aerobics class advertises for all ages, the trainers do have to be on the vetting database; but if the class is 'targeted' at adults and children come along, the trainers do not have to be on the database.
- A self-employed tennis coach does not have to be checked, but if he takes on a volunteer the volunteer would have to be checked.

The biggest danger of all is that within the bowels of these great state databases exist all sorts of inaccurate, irrelevant, subjective and intrusive information about us, which we may not even know exists because the data is hidden. The CRB includes 'soft information' such as police suspicions and speculation along with information about incidents when someone has been questioned but released. When criminal records are public we know what the police are recording. Is it right that such 'soft intelligence' (which can be nothing more than unfounded gossip, rumour and speculation) is put on our criminal record?

Take the example of a Sunday-school teacher, a mother of five, who was given a police record after she briefly left her four children playing together in a park while she visited a nearby shop with the fifth child to buy them all ice cream. When she returned minutes later she found the police talking to her children. The woman, from Warminster, Wiltshire, who asked not to be named, told the *Daily Telegraph* in an article published on 14 July 2009: 'The police made a snap judgement on my parenting, that's all it is. I haven't committed any criminal offence. It's just a snap judgement after meeting me for a minute or two in the park.'

She wasn't arrested but unbeknown to her the 'incident' was logged with the Criminal Records Bureau and she was labelled as a risk to children! She only learned of her 'criminal record' after applying for a voluntary job teaching at her church's Sunday school.

Secrecy is the means and the justification for collecting and storing such subjective and intrusive personal data. Let's not be fooled by the apparatchiks that this secrecy protects us. The reality is that nothing puts us in more danger – as my final story illustrates.

Criminalising complaint

One of the most disturbing things I came across while writing this book was the discovery that in councils across Britain there exist secret registers of 'violent offenders' and 'potential violent offenders'. What is interesting about these databases is that they comprise, in the main, people who have not actually committed any physical violence. Instead they are people who, in the entirely subjective opinion of a council official, have the *potential* to be violent.

Jane Clift is one of these people. She doesn't look violent and nor is she. She's a 43-year-old woman[3] who expects people to do the jobs they are paid by the public to do. Jane has never been in trouble with the police but rather takes an active interest in her community, the sort of person politicians always claim they want to engage.

Jane was walking in her local park in August 2005 when she saw a three-year-old boy trampling through a flower bed, uprooting flowers and pulling the heads off plants. Jane phoned the council and asked for a park warden to come by, but none arrived. She then approached a group of nearby adults and asked them whether this was their child. When one of the women replied that it was her son, Jane asked that she stop him destroying the flower bed as it was there for everyone to enjoy. Some might say Jane was brave or foolish to make an approach on her own, but that would be to buy into the state's propaganda that we are not capable of engaging with our fellow citizens directly. One of these adults was drunk and abusive and in response to Jane's request to stop the child destroying the flower bed, he jumped in and started smashing it up himself. Jane called the police.

The police took about forty minutes to arrive. The adults had left but Jane followed them at a distance to see where they went and took note of the address. She also took the names and addresses of two witnesses. Maybe few of us would be this active, but I would say Jane's determination to hold these

3. I can't help noticing the state's predilection for bullying middle-aged women, or is it simply that these women, by being such sympathetic people, have a better chance of shaming public officials for their intimidatory tactics? I'd be interested to hear from anyone else similarly intimidated by the state, middle-aged, female or otherwise.

people to account is more admirable than not. When the police arrived they apologised for the delay but despite Jane's ample evidence they told her there was nothing they could do because the amount of damage was monetarily minimal. They advised her instead to call Slough Borough Council's antisocial behaviour unit as the council had recently launched a campaign stating how it was getting tough on this sort of crime.

When Jane got home she called the parks manager, Colin Bailey, who also referred her to the antisocial behaviour unit, in particular a woman named Fozia Rashid. (Now already this is *too much bureaucracy*. Even the name 'antisocial behaviour' is a euphemism – either something is a crime or it is not. If it's a crime then the criminal justice system needs to deal with it quickly and efficiently. That's why we pay for it. If it's not dealing with crime, what is the point?)

By now most of us would have given up in frustration but Jane was determined. She wanted at least one public servant to do the job he or she was paid to do. Why have all these people if the end result is no action? She expected the council to at least look into the incident, visit the parents responsible or view the damage to the flower bed.

But when Jane telephoned Fozia Rashid the next day, 11 August 2005, the woman was dismissive. She said the council could not take action simply because a child had been 'picking flowers' and if the man had committed criminal damage this was a matter between Jane Clift and the police, even though Jane explained how the police had said it was a council matter. Rashid said no action would be taken because 'these things happen all the time'. When Jane asked how this attitude squared with the council's stated zero tolerance on antisocial behaviour, Rashid said words to the effect that 'no action could be taken in respect of the anti-social behaviour because you were the cause of it'.

Jane Clift could barely speak, but demanded to know what Rashid meant by such a comment. The woman responded: 'Why did you stay in the park for forty minutes? Why did you follow them home? You were provoking them. You should have left the area.'

Jane was doing exactly what the council claimed it wanted people to do – report antisocial behaviour – and for her trouble *she* was being criticised rather than the person who actually committed the physical damage. Clearly anyone who tries to solve a problem directly, without the state's inter-vention, is likely to be seen as a threat to the state's all-pervasive power. Even more of a threat than the actual person committing the criminal damage.

Jane was outraged but defended herself by asking what kind of society would it be if everyone just walked away – is that what the council was advocating? Rashid then said Jane was being abusive and in her frustration Jane slammed down the phone.

Fortunately for Jane, she had this conversation while her friend Mohammed Gulfraz was in the room, and because it was on speakerphone he heard everything. Gulfraz is a 56-year-old family man, a citizen of Slough for some forty years and a council-tax payer.

After the injustice of being blamed for someone else's crim-inal activity, Jane phoned the council to make a complaint. An official in the Corporate Complaints Department told her she could not lodge a complaint because the flower beds belonged to the council – not her – and it was up to them what they did. This refusal just to record her complaint angered her even more. She was told the only way to sort out the matter was to speak to Fozia Rashid again. Jane explained that Ms Rashid was useless and she had no wish to speak to her again and that she could drop down dead.

That was an expression of her frustration. Jane then wrote a letter of complaint outlining what had taken place. She sent it to the council and to the press. She wanted the wider public to know what had happened. I bet you know what's coming next. If you've read Chapter 2 you know how much money councils spend pumping out propaganda and what they hate more than anything is unauthorised information getting into the public domain to contradict their official, feel-good stories of smiling, competent workers. In her letter Jane described what had happened and her feeling of outrage at the way she'd been treated by the council. She 'felt so affronted and so filled with anger that I am certain I would have physically attacked her [Rashid] if she had been anywhere near me. I truly am not of that nature and so, surely, this should act as a wake-up call to the borough as to the capacity she had for offending people'. No one thought this was anything more than a colourful expression, one most of us use, particularly when dealing with obstructive officialdom. Certainly the council didn't take it as a serious threat of violence as no one complained until three and a half months later.

On 24 August 2005 the *Slough Observer* published an article, 'Standing up to vandalism', relating Jane's story. It quoted an unnamed council 'spokesman'[4] as saying: 'We are very grateful and thank Ms Clift for bringing the vandalism to our attention and the parks department will be issuing

4. Another instance where anonymity has granted an official immunity from what transpired to be an outright lie.

a formal report to the police which could bring about a possible prosecution for criminal damage.'

In fact, no report was ever produced.

Now it's time to introduce a new character to this bizarre little drama. His name is Patrick Kelleher and he was at the time Slough Borough Council's 'Head of Public Protection' (brace yourself for how he interpreted this job title). When Jane's complaint was palmed off on yet another council staffer who attempted to close the matter down by telling Jane there would be an internal investigation and appropriate (i.e. no) action taken, Jane wrote to the council again. Patrick Kelleher was put in charge of investigating Jane's complaint. He invited Jane for a meeting on 25 October and while sipping coffee in Wellington House Jane repeated her complaint against Fozia Rashid and her frustration that not only did the woman do nothing but she had the gall to blame Jane for the incident. The next day Kelleher wrote to Jane Clift, and it's important to note his language in this letter in relation to what he did next: 'May I take this opportunity to thank you for attending yesterday's meeting at Wellington House to discuss your various concerns ... a meeting which I found extremely helpful.' There was no suggestion from Kelleher that he thought Jane was threatening or violent.

Then Kelleher went to interview Rashid, who accused Jane of shouting at her. This accusation was not backed up by anyone else and was not in agreement with the only witness to the conversation, Mr Gulfraz. Nonetheless, it was at this point that Kelleher changed tack. Some might say the council closed ranks.

For it was after this conversation that Kelleher switched the focus of his investigation from Fozia Rashid, the council employee, to Jane Clift, the citizen. Now let's remember that

Kelleher was supposed to be investigating Jane's complaint that Rashid had done absolutely nothing when told of an actual incident of antisocial behaviour. He discovered this was the case – Rashid had taken no action whatsoever, despite the council's well-funded advertising campaign urging citizens to report such crimes to the council. So if nothing else, she should have been disciplined for failing to do her taxpayer-funded job. But that was not the Slough Council way. Kelleher decided instead to follow Rashid's lead and blame it all on Jane Clift. He rejected his own interview notes, denounced Mr Gulfraz as a 'stooge' and then claimed that he was entitled to, and did, disregard Gulfraz's witness statement. On 30 November 2005 he wrote to Jane: 'In line with the Directorate's Violence at Work Policy . . . I am writing to inform you that because of your behaviour towards Ms Rashid a warning marker will be placed against your name for a period of 18 months. The warning marker will also be shared with other council departments and government agencies within the borough, by electronic or manual means.'

Jane was deemed a 'medium'-level threat – the same as violent criminals and those who attempt sexual assault – and her listing was then circulated to a wide range of public and private bodies, including doctors, dentists, opticians, libraries, contraceptive clinics, schools, nurseries and fifty town centre businesses. Their staff were advised not to see her alone and Jane, who was in the process of applying to be a foster-parent, had to withdraw her application.

'It is terrifying that there is almost no proof required and no hearing to determine the truth of the allegation,' Jane told me. 'It could happen to anybody who gets into even the most minor disagreement with their council and who won't be fobbed off by inadequate and partisan complaint handling. I am a very quiet, mild-mannered person by nature and the way these inept, complicit and remorseless council jobsworths treated me was reprehensible. They are totally out of control and yet apparently this infamous council does not propose even to hold an inquiry into the conduct and competence of its staff.'

Like most of us, Jane couldn't understand how a council could so easily blacken her good name without any evidence and without giving her the right to a fair hearing. What about the data protection law? Wasn't that meant to protect an individual's privacy from the power of the state? She queried Slough's data protection/health and safety manager Peter Satterthwaite but was told only: 'When a customer is abusive or aggressive, we have no option than to place the customer on a register for a set period commensurate with behaviour or actions.'

Actually, there is another option: if a crime has been committed, report it to the police and let justice take its course. Why else are we paying for the criminal justice system if not to deal with criminal behaviour? Instead, secrecy and the failures of the criminal justice system have instigated an entire culture of secret summary justice that is spreading throughout the public institutions of Britain.

With all the lack of logic we've come to expect from a bureaucracy, Slough's guidance states that for the following 'crimes' employees must fill out a violent incident form: shouting, swearing, racial or sexual abuse, threats, pushing, spitting, object thrown, damage, hostage. However, for actual violence they *don't* fill out a violence form but a corporate incident form.

CRIME AND PUNISHMENT

Line managers will investigate the incident and implement any measures necessary to avoid another occurrence.

Victims will be offered counselling and, if appropriate, legal assistance may well be available. The line manager will initially instigate these services by contacting the COHSU for advice and assistance.

PVP classification

Below is a list of activities that may render a person liable to have a violent person's marker placed on their file for a set period, and covered by this code of practice. The set period will be commensurate with the activity.

Activity	Set Period	Activity	Set Period
◊ Shouting / Swearing	3 months	◊ Spitting	15 months + special conditions
◊ Racial Abuse	6 months	◊ Object Thrown	18 months + special conditions
◊ Sexual Abuse	6 months	◊ Damage	18 months + special conditions
◊ Threats	1 year	◊ Hostage	2 years + special conditions
◊ Pushing	15 months + special conditions	◊ Violence	3 years + special conditions

Special conditions include but not limited to - ban / appointment visits only / injunction etc – as determined appropriate by the Service Head.

The timescale will be increased by three times if the perpetrator commits a further offence during the set period.

Internally generated incident forms

Each section that has dealings with the public, within the directorate, will nominate a PVP controller. This person is responsible for maintaining a folder containing Violent Incident reports in a secure manner, but at the same time ensuring that staff that may have future dealings with a perpetrator (or the address where an incident occurred) are duly warned before the visit / meeting.

Note how the council refers to the person challenging the official as 'the perpetrator', making it entirely plain how the council sees itself as judge and jury. If Slough Borough Council actually thought Jane was violent then why did it take nearly four months for it to see her as a threat? The plain fact is the council didn't like Jane Clift complaining and pointing out that a council official was not doing her job and they saw it as their right to spend taxpayer money persecuting her.

This is all depressingly familiar. What happened next, though, breaks all convention of English citizen serfdom and gives me hope because if you fight back you very often win. It may seem easier when confronted by officialdom simply to give in, lay low, surrender, but bureaucrats are like blackmailers and the more you give the more they'll demand. It's only by standing up to these demands that they slow and maybe even stop.

Jane sued the council for libel, claiming they had defamed her. I love this – she takes the world's most draconian libel law (traditionally the tool only for rich litigious bullies around the globe) and uses it against a bullying council. Not only that – she wins! I just happened to randomly come across Jane while I was visiting the High Court during the summer of 2009 and sat in on her hearing. I don't imagine her case is an anomaly. By the time I'd heard what Slough Council had done to her, I was ready to break out some pompoms and give Jane a cheer. Yay for Jane! The jury, too, found in Jane's favour and though she was not able to prove the council acted with malicious intent in libelling her (an almost impossible thing to prove), Mr Justice Tugendhat ordered Slough to pay the legal costs of the case, estimated at between £300,000 and £400,000 and compensation of £12,000. This, however, was four years after the initial incident and it had been a long, hard road. Slough Borough Council plans to appeal the ruling and spend yet more public money.

What both Sally Murrer's and Jane Clift's cases reveal is the lengths to which the state will go in pursuing individuals who challenge its authority. The police, councils and other public bodies are spending vast amounts of our money pummelling us with propaganda and persecuting those who dare question their view of reality. I have highlighted two of the more high-profile cases; there are thousands of others that remain secret. The 'lives of others' is now the main preoccupation of officialdom, and none of us should sleep easier for that. We are not made safer by this but ever more vulnerable to unfounded gossip, rumour and speculation.

Unlimited public funds, unaccountability and anonymity all lead to one thing – never having to say you're sorry. And that is precisely what you can see in the response from Thames Valley Police and Slough Borough Council. They refuse to accept blame; even now they won't admit they did anything wrong – that is the scariest thing of all. Instead, they follow the PR pattern of throwing *our* money at the problem, continuing to litigate and pursue paths which everyone can see are dead ends and a waste of precious public resource. Slough hasn't disciplined *any* of the officials involved and instead plans to appeal the High Court decision while Thames Valley Police maintain they did nothing wrong.

The irony is that all these efforts to make us safer – or at least to make us feel safer – simply end up criminalising more people. Restricting public access to criminal records and incident reports benefits the state because it means avoiding public scrutiny while charging usurious rates for what should be public information.

In our PR-obsessed age of total information control, officials view the release of any unauthorised information, however inconsequential, as a crime worthy of persecution and prosecution. The aim of such intimidation is to show the common man the utter destruction that can be made of his life if he dares speak against the state.

Why do we accept this sorry state of affairs? We don't have to. The successes of Jane and Sally show what any ordinary person can do if they put their mind to it. Why let these petty jobsworths ruin our lives? Our country? These women are doing their part to challenge the system and make it reflect the will of the citizenry. They are not rich in resources or carrying an address book packed full of elite connections, yet they took on the powerful state and won.

Which brings me to one final story. You might have heard about it.

8

Bringing Down the House

We're all tightly packed on the green leather benches of the House of Commons. I'm chatting to a fellow MP who holds his order papers. A man on the floor rises and makes an announcement. The murmuring stops. We listen intently and then suddenly a name is announced and it's pandemonium. All around me suited men and women are hollering and cheering. 'Hear! hear!' 'Well done, Michael.' The raucous revelry is infectious; despite myself, I cheer too. Everyone on the Labour benches is going crazy.

The new Speaker is 'dragged' past me – one of those quaint parliamentary traditions whereby he is gently manhandled by two fellow MPs towards the Speaker's chair. We whoop and cheer some more. I shout 'Hear! hear!' in my best English accent. The blue-eyed, bewigged clerks seated at the large central table with the dispatch boxes allow themselves a wry smile. The Speaker shakes hands with one of the clerks and ascends the steps to the big chair where he takes his place at the very heart of this, the mother of all parliaments. 'Order! Order!' he says, the first of many times he will utter such words.

It's all so grand in the Commons chamber, it's no wonder so many MPs become puffed up with pomposity. All those clerks and policemen running around outside scolding members of the public for sitting in the wrong seats (which they have paid for).

In here the public have to make do with the view from the fixed cameras or the public gallery, which is encased in bullet-proof plastic. These benches are solely the preserve of the political elite, like an old gentlemen's club. There are rows of heraldic shields and gilded portcullis icons. I tap one of the ribbons of filigreed vines on my bench and hear an unexpectedly hollow sound. What is it? Cheap plastic? Not quite the quality I'd expected. The green benches are more cramped, too, and some of these MPs look strangely familiar. I rest back on the seat looking up at the ceiling towards the public and press galleries. But they are fore-shortened and the ceiling is decorated not with Gothic carvings but rain-stained sheets of plywood. From metal rafters hang six large silk lanterns blazing like suns, known in the trade as 'space lights'.

This is what they mean by the magic of movies – something designed to fool the camera but unable to withstand close personal inspection (a bit like many politicians in that respect). You've twigged by now – I'm not in the real House of Commons, just as I'm not a real MP. Instead I'm on the set of *On Expenses* (originally titled *Bringing Down the House*), the BBC film being made about my part in the MPs' expenses scandal. This is only a replica of the House of

Commons[1] chamber, the only one in the UK, built originally by Granada Television in their Manchester studios for
The New Statesman featuring Alan B'Stard, then bought by
a set designer and moved out here to a barn in the middle
of the Oxford countryside. Outside these doors the only self-
important, puffed-up creature you'll find is a rooster or two.
It's December and we've been told to dress warmly as the
barn is unheated and the green carpet still soggy, as until
last night it was under two inches of water. The industrial
heaters blast between takes.

I've tried my best to dress dowdily in a simple black suit
to take my place among the other MPs who are a collection
of extras made up of supporting artists, writers, and half
the executives of BBC Northern Ireland Drama who are
producing the film. In this scene we're jubilant as our man
Michael Martin has just been selected as the new Speaker.
It's not without some irony, I think, that I'm cast as an MP
cheering on the appointment of the man who did the most
to stymie my campaign to open up Parliament to the people.
'The Speaker's revenge,' chuckles the actor Brian Cox, who
is playing the Glaswegian MP. I've never actually met Michael
Martin but if he was as charming as Brian Cox I'm pretty
certain I would not be here today asking for a photo with
his thespian double.

'How about sitting on his lap?' says the director, always
looking for a good *mise en scène*. 'Speaker's Little Helper.'

1. The serjeant-at-arms refused to allow the BBC to film inside Parliament
for what was originally titled *The Heather Brooke Story*. Even requests to
film outside were initially denied despite similar requests being approved
for less critical fare. Getting footage of the empty Commons chamber was
denied, too, despite cameras (paid for by us) trained on the green seats.

He laughs. It is December after all, and with all his make-up and wigged white hair Cox does bear some resemblance to Santa. Wary of looking foolish but feeling festive, I agree – so I now have a quite risqué photo of myself draped across the Speaker's lap. Maybe I'll send it round to Martin next Christmas. Brighten up his office in the Lords.

It's quite surreal having a film made about your life. A costume director came round to study my wardrobe. I recorded my voice for the actress Anna Maxwell Martin so she could hear my strange transatlantic accent and later I watched her playing me in the Royal Courts of Justice while 150 people stood around doing whatever it is film people do. I'm proud of my part in the disclosures of MPs' abuse of their expenses. We needed this to happen. What we had before was not democracy. It is not democratic for elected officials to claim public money to build up a property empire and then refuse to tell the public anything about it. It is not democratic to expect the taxpayer to live by one set of rules while those who make the rules live by another.

When I started off on this path I wasn't expecting to bring a plague on all politicians' houses. I was merely doing field research for my first book, *Your Right to Know*, a citizens' guide to the UK's then new Freedom of Information Act. I was replicating a story I'd done in Washington State back in 1992 as a young reporter where I'd asked my local politicians for all their expense receipts and received them in a matter of days. The MPs' expenses scandal became such a huge event only because parliamentarians tried for too long to live in the past. They refused to treat the public with respect, thinking nothing of taking the people's money, foisting a barrage of laws upon them and then shutting the doors of Parliament and living a life they denied the rest of us, free from their own laws, subsidising their lifestyle at taxpayer expense while remaining unaccountable to all but their political party bosses.

Ever since I read George Orwell's *Nineteen Eighty-four* at the age of eighteen I've been passionate about holding the powerful to account. I pine for a return to the type of old-school journalism made popular by Ben Hecht in films and plays depicting the tough newspapermen and -women of the 1930s. Being nosy, seeking justice, pricking the pompous and, above all, challenging the powerful – that's my idea of fun. Moats and duck houses, bell towers and bath plugs: it wasn't exactly how I envisioned the big story of my career. I don't recall Dustin Hoffman in *All the President's Men* poring through receipts of porn movies and country manor houses (he had a much more serious Deep Throat keeping him busy). But while the trivia titillates, there were similar principles at stake about the people's right to know how their elected officials spent public money and exercised power. The unexpurgated details of MPs' second homes allowances revealed more than just petty eccentricities. They showed mortgages being claimed for houses that had already been paid off; MPs flipping house designations to maximise tax avoidance; others building up entire property portfolios at taxpayers' expense. All indicative of an overall attitude of entitlement to the public's money.

Back in 2004, when I began this investigation, I had no idea I was starting out on a five-year legal battle that would end up in the High Court and culminate in the resignation of the first Speaker of the House of Commons in three hundred years, along with the resignation of half a dozen ministers and scores of MPs standing down at the next election. I certainly hadn't predicted Parliament would react in the arrogant way it did to my requests, with officials and MPs digging their heels in and doing everything humanly possible to stop not just democracy but the entire Internet and information revolution. It was that unfathomable stubbornness that riled me. The more they disdainfully refused my requests, the more determined I became to break open this feudal and secretive institution.

As part of my book research, I had written to all sorts of public institutions asking about preparations for the new Freedom of Information Act that was coming into force in January 2005. I had also put in a number of requests under the voluntary Code of Practice on Access to Government Information asking for things I thought should be readily available to people and yet were off-limits.

FOI may seem an odd thing to campaign about (certainly no one understood what I was up to for a long time), but if you're at all interested in power, access to information is key. We cannot call ourselves an informed electorate without information. It follows that we need information to understand decisions, to participate in policymaking, to be true citizens in a democracy. I also believe in free access to official information because it enables a different style of politics. Instead of public-schoolboy posturing and point-scoring it allows people to study an issue in a much less divisive, confrontational way. FOI gives people the ability to get involved in politics without being political, and that was exactly what I wanted to do.

The reason: I was fed up with the place where I was living.

I've already mentioned my antipathy to Tower Hamlets Council and this is when it began, in 2002. At the time I was living in Bethnal Green with my husband on an ex-council estate. It was our first home, a beautiful old Victorian flat in a conservation area, but unfortunately it was surrounded by people who treated the neighbourhood like a dump. The council spent thousands of pounds on posters in twelve different languages but when I called the police to report a crime no one ever appeared. Gangs of boys prowled our stairwells dealing drugs, threatening women, leaving litter everywhere and yet no one did anything. Not one thing. You could call the police: nothing. You could call the council: nothing.

I couldn't understand it. I thought there was some procedure I wasn't getting. I went to all the council's talking shops looking for answers. The officials were all very helpful up until the point when I pressed them for hard detailed facts and specific action. How many sexual assaults had occurred on my street? They refused to tell me. When an American artist of my own age named Margaret Muller was stabbed to death while jogging at 8.30 a.m. in nearby Victoria Park I wanted to know how many other attacks had been reported previously. Again, they wouldn't tell me. How many 999 calls did the police get and how many did they fail to attend? No answer. The only thing on offer was CCTV cameras but when I asked how many people were arrested and convicted using footage, they didn't know. Why not put the money into actual police doing actual police work? I queried. But that clearly wasn't fashionable. I stopped calling the police, and eventually accepted what my husband had long been telling me: that there was no point. It was mind-numbingly frustrating, but made me realise that something had to be done.

What most outraged me about all my dealings with public institutions was the attitude held by most officials that only they could be trusted with real information and real power. The public couldn't. All this rhetoric about 'engaging the local community' seemed to comprise handing out benefits. I couldn't square in my mind the plethora of official leaflets urging people to 'claim the max' from their fellow citizens' hard-earned income while these same officials refused to provide the sort of information and power that would allow people to take control of their lives in a real, meaningful way that could make them independent of state welfare.

I was nearly done with my book when I decided in January 2004 to phone up the Houses of Parliament to ask about MPs' expenses. At that time only the main switchboard number had been made public, and when I called, I was disconcerted that the operator couldn't find any listing related to freedom of information. (Although the Freedom of Information Act had been passed in 2000 its implementation was put off until 1 January 2005, the longest 'preparation' time in the world, which gives an indication of how our dear leaders embraced the people's right to know.) When I finally found the person in charge of FOI, I explained that one of the things I was after was a breakdown of MPs' expenses by receipt. After a baffled silence, the woman on the phone said they would look into it. A few weeks later I received an email telling me that all MPs' expenses would be published in October 2004.

Success?

Not quite.

What came out in October 2004 were bulk figures in various categories: travel, staff, second homes, etc. I wanted the detail. I wanted actual receipts. That's where you find the truth. The reason I was so intent on receipts, and so certain that they existed, is very simple: I'd seen them before.

My first proper job as a reporter was as an intern covering the Washington State legislature in 1992 for that state's second-largest newspaper. My editor could see I wanted to get stuck into something more meaty than just the daily round of committee hearings and debates. It was a bad recession in the newspaper business at that time (though nothing like the decimation of the industry now) and I needed an investigative story to help me land my next job. He suggested I look at our local politicians' expense claims. It was a common and perennial story that resurfaced every few years, though it was new to me. I went to the clerk's office and made my request. Surprisingly, I was told that these items were part of the public record in Washington so I could inspect them at any time. I set myself up in one of the small rooms in the clerk's office and they brought me boxes full of receipts: airline tickets, hotel and room-service bills, mileage claims. When I sat in that office in the state capitol of Olympia I was left to my own devices. The officials were there to answer any questions but mostly they just went about their business. There was no suspicion or hostility; the public servants understood my role as a reporter and accepted that even if I were critical I was a necessary part of democracy. If they minded me being in their office going through the files they never let on. (I've been in a similar position in British public bureaucracies on a few occasions, and each time I was watched like a criminal by some hostile and paranoid official.

I spent a day or so going through all the receipts. I was interested to see how the system worked but I was also keeping an eye out for any questionable claims. Imagine my disappointment when all these hours of investigation failed to uncover a single improper claim! The only dubious thing about the entire system was that frequent-flyer miles accrued during official business trips went to the private individual. That became my first big 'investigative' story. Even if it didn't set the world on fire, this exercise taught me something fundamental about the power of transparency. It keeps those in power honest: more than any regulator, more than any bureaucracy or set of rules. Simply knowing that the people who elect you will be able to see what you're up to is enough to chasten even the most greedy, power-mongering politician. I moved on to work as a general assignment reporter and a crime reporter at other newspapers but I always liked delving into bureaucracy. I did a big story about the state of South Carolina's crime lab and how delays in forensic evidence were leading to miscarriages of justice, and exposed the way funeral homes were run with almost no accountability. Both these investigations led to changes in state law.

As time went by, and I covered murder after murder, I realised I'd had enough. I found myself, at twenty-six, completely burned out, so I left for Britain – birthplace of my parents – to get away from journalism altogether. But then I moved to Tower Hamlets and discovered all it took to reignite my investigative passion was the infuriating truculence, and secrecy, of British bureaucrats. I kept asking myself: what were they so afraid of us knowing?

Fast forward to October 2004, and while I'd found some officials to be helpful in providing information, those in the Commons were surprisingly secretive. They argued that to publish the details of MPs' allowances would be an unfair invasion of their privacy. I pointed out that the allowances could only be claimed for items that were 'wholly, exclusively and necessarily incurred in the course of performing parliamentary duties', so there should be nothing private about them. But the authorities seemed to find it inconceivable that an outsider should be allowed to trawl through a Right Honourable Member's claims. Not only did they refuse to publish the claims and receipts of MPs' expenses, they would not even tell me the procedures used to record expenses. This made me suspicious. Why were they so reluctant to explain unless they knew the system wouldn't stand up to public scrutiny?

As soon as the FOI law came into force in January 2005 I filed my first freedom-of-information request to the House of Commons. Initially I asked for the names and salaries of MPs' staff because it was rumoured that many MPs had relatives on the payroll who did little to no work. The only way to check was to know that person's name and salary. The best people to police the system are constituents themselves (not a parliamentary regulator) because it is the constituents who have the most dealings with MPs' staff and know if they are actually doing the work they are paid to do. The political and investigative reporter Michael Crick was one of the people I interviewed for *Your Right to Know* and he explained to me the opacity by which MPs could pay family members from the public purse with absolutely no public documentation about who they were or the work they were supposedly doing. This struck me as the sort of unaccountable behaviour common to a banana republic and not what I'd expected from Parliament. When I looked into it I found it exactly as Michael had described: MPs were simply drawing funds from the public purse without providing any sort of accountability.

Need I mention this request was rejected? Undeterred, I appealed to the Information Commissioner, who is the regulator for both freedom of information and data protection (privacy). More than a year later he made a decision to uphold the status quo but only because his hand was forced by the Speaker of the House, Michael Martin. Martin had signed a certificate stating that disclosure of the names of MPs' staff would be 'likely to prejudice the effective conduct of public affairs' and would also endanger their 'health and safety'. No evidence was put forward for these speculations, nothing except the certificate signed by Martin, which was considered conclusive evidence. It was an absolute exemption under the UK's FOI law and there was no public interest test and no way I could see to appeal. This is how a theocracy operates, not a democracy. End of the road on that one, but I made sure a few newspapers knew about Martin's draconian action.

I made another request in 2006, this time for a breakdown of MPs' travel claims. It too was rejected. I didn't appeal this one as the MP Norman Baker had a similar request already with the Information Commissioner. In March 2006 I asked for a detailed breakdown of all MPs' additional costs allowances (ACA). These are claims of up to £24,000 that an MP can claim on a second home. It can be either his main home or constituency home and often the two are equidistant from Parliament. While initially the expense was designed to help MPs from distant constituencies attend Parliament, it had become a cash cow and a way for an MP to build up a property empire on the taxpayer.

Again, this request was refused citing the Data Protection Act. Let's remember this law was passed to protect the privacy of private citizens yet here were MPs – who had done more than anyone to strip private people of their privacy – hijacking the law to shield themselves from being publicly accountable for how they were spending public money in the course of their public duties. Their exact words were: *The disclosure of anything more detailed than a bulk figure would be 'unfair' to MPs*. I appealed to the Information Commissioner, determined to highlight MPs' blazing hypocrisy. The Commons then came up with another excuse – it would cost too much to disclose to the public how MPs were spending public money. To any sensible person this is ludicrous but the commissioner accepted this and so I was forced to narrow my request to an acceptable limit determined by the House of Commons. They decided I could only ask for ten MPs' expenses from a total of 646. So on 30 November 2006, nearly three years after that first call to the Houses of Parliament's switchboard, I refiled my request asking for the detailed second homes expenses of ten MPs – including all the party leaders – and waited.

A few weeks later, on 18 December, Tory backbencher David Maclean quietly introduced the Freedom of Information (Amendment) Bill which would exempt the

House of Commons and Lords from their own law. The cited reason was to 'protect constituents' privacy'. Good one, David! As we know now, the real aim was to stop constituents knowing about MPs' expenses. This disingenuousness should remind us why it is important to maintain extreme scepticism whenever any politician carps on about wanting to 'protect our privacy'. Most likely he has something of his own he's keen to hide. Maclean's stated purpose for proposing this outrageously undemocratic bill: 'When we write on behalf of constituents . . . we must be able to look them in the eye and say that in all circumstances what they tell us will not get out,' he told MPs. 'It is like the relationship with a priest. We will write to an authority with their problem, but we guarantee that that information will not be leaked by us, or get into the public domain.'

Isn't that good of him, this public servant, to look out for his constituents? Fact is, this was a completely made-up problem that had *never, ever occurred*. This is the sort of disaster-movie scenario the authorities often dream up when attempting to put an acceptable public face on their own insidious desire to hide questionable activities. I immediately put in an FOI request asking for the number of times constituents' correspondence had been published under FOI. The answer, as I'd suspected, was zero. Privacy law would prevent this anyway, so it was clear 'privacy' was simply the ruse by which MPs hoped to fool the public into granting themselves an exemption from their own FOI law.

Most private members' bills start life with virtually no chance of becoming law unless they have government backing, and as this one came from the opposition it should have died a quick death. Amazingly, however, it sailed through not just one but *two* readings entirely unopposed. The day of the second reading, 19 January 2007, just happened to be one of big news: Ruth Turner, the senior Downing Street aide in the cash-for-honours investigation, had just been arrested. When it was put to David Maclean that he'd chosen to put his bill at the very end of a busy parliamentary day, he told the *Guardian*: 'I am showing some of the younger hands how you can get a bill through Parliament after long experience as a whip in both getting and blocking bills through Parliament.'

A group of cross-party MPs, led by Liberal Democrat Norman Baker, tried to derail the bill by talking it out. Baker and his fellow supporters heroically talked for the full five hours allocated to private members' bills so that the bill could not be voted upon and moved to the Lords. They managed to kill it off twice using this tactic but each time, miraculously, it was resurrected. Finally in May 2007 the bill went through with an unprecedented number of votes for a Friday afternoon (when most MPs are in their constituencies): 96 MPs in favour, 25 against.

A press campaign saw reporters from all papers coming out against the treacherous bill. It was highly effective and I wish we saw more campaigns like this, with the media working together to further the common aim of freedom of information and expression. All this campaigning was not in vain because the bill ultimately could not find a sponsor in the House of Lords. Rather, it was branded a 'scandalous' piece of legislation and Maclean was forced to retreat.[2] It's quite clear to me that this bill could not have

2. Maclean remained, however, a member of the Members Estimate Committee in charge of reviewing MPs' expenses.

got as far as it had without specific ministerial backing, particularly from the prime minister. Throughout this sorry saga, a PM committed to transparency and the public's right to know would not have put up with such shenanigans. Instead we see a PM pulling the strings to shut out the public but keeping himself one step removed so he can all the while deny responsibility.

By this time my amended FOI request for the ten MPs' expenses had been rejected (again on privacy grounds) and on 13 June 2007 the Information Commissioner made his ruling on my appeal. His decision was an attempt at compromise but in being so it pleased no one.

> The Commissioner decided that the requested information is personal data and that its fully itemised disclosure would be unfair. However he has decided that it would not contravene the data protection principles to disclose information showing the totals paid under specified headings within the Additional Costs Allowance.

He then arbitrarily created categories such as mortgage, rent, security, food, etc. But this was not how the Fees Office in Parliament recorded the data and would have necessitated a huge amount of work, much more than simply publishing the raw receipts. It didn't satisfy me either as I wanted those receipts, convinced by this point that a myriad of sins were hiding behind the aggregate totals. The Commons appealed to the Information Tribunal. Meanwhile, I discovered there were two other journalists with FOI requests similar to mine. I contacted them both. Jonathan Ungoed-Thomas from the

Sunday Times was a reporter whom I'd talked to at various times about FOI requests. He was not confident in the appeals process, having experienced already the chronic delays and lack of enforcement typical of this regulator.[3] I couldn't disagree with him but I was stubborn enough to keep going. I then phoned Ben Leapman at the *Sunday Telegraph*. We went to lunch and he was keen to appeal but was wary of doing so on his own. We agreed to pool resources.

You don't need legal representation to appeal to the Information Tribunal but it helps, particularly when you're taking on the Establishment, as they come with a posse of taxpayer-funded lawyers. Fortunately, as a writer and campaigner on FOI, I meet quite a lot of lawyers. One of them was the barrister Hugh Tomlinson QC, who was intrigued by my ability to 'cause trouble' as he put it. I'd met him at my first Information Tribunal in December 2006 when I was battling (funnily enough) the BBC. I was seeking the minutes of the governors' meeting in which former director general Greg Dyke had resigned after the Hutton Inquiry. Hugh was representing the *Guardian* in that case while I represented myself. We had stayed in touch and at the launch of the second edition of *Your Right to Know* Hugh offered to represent me pro bono if I should again find

3. The problem remains serious. According to the Campaign for Freedom of Information it takes on average 19.7 months from the date a complaint is received by the commissioner to his making a decision. The average investigation into a complaint does not even begin until eight months after the complaint has been received. In 28 per cent of cases, there was a delay of more than a year before the investigation began. By that time, most information is no longer useful or valid.

myself before the Information Tribunal. I wasn't sure how valid this offer was as it's a rare lawyer who offers to work pro bono, but in the summer of 2007 I decided to find out. I outlined my case to him. Was he interested? In short, he was, even chuckling that it would probably be 'good fun' (how right he was).

We began preparing for the hearing, and Ben and I discussed our strategy. I came at it using my outsider's perspective, as a foreigner who had seen receipts released elsewhere with nothing but good results for democracy and accountability. I looked at the system in place in Scotland where *Sunday Herald* reporter Paul Hutcheon had brought about wholesale reform through his FOI requests to the Scottish Parliament. The Scottish Information Commissioner had already ruled that MSPs must disclose all their expense receipts as a result of Paul's requests, giving us an important legal precedent. I also studied cases in Europe and America. In November 2007, Jonathan Ungoed-Thomas and the *Sunday Times* decided to join our appeal. In total we were now asking for the receipts of fourteen MPs.

When I went into the two-day hearing on 7 February 2008, I was immensely grateful to have Hugh Tomlinson with me as it was lawyers to the right of me, and lawyers to the left: a real lawyer beanfeast all paid for by the taxpayer, with the majority there to stop the taxpayer finding out how their taxes were being spent. There were lawyers and officials from the House of Commons, the Treasury Solicitor's Office (providing taxpayer-funded legal advice to government) and the Information Commissioner's Office. The only people *not* being funded by the taxpayer were those of us attempting to find out how public money was being spent, i.e. myself and the two other journalists. In fact, the small tribunal room in London's Bedford Square was so full of lawyers there wasn't any room for me! I wasn't about to take a back seat in my own case so when I spotted an empty chair with papers on the desk I made a dash for it.

We are in court 1, a small subterranean room of magnolia tint with fluorescent lights in metal grilles, one of which is flickering its death throes. The tables and chairs look like a job lot from IKEA. A tall man looms over me. 'You've moved my papers.' He has an icy posh accent, the kind one often hears from the mouths of Hollywood villains. This, it transpires, is Mr Andrew Walker himself, the director of Parliament's Department of Resources, or the Fees Office as it is more commonly known. He reminds me of Eric Morecambe and wears – what else – a grey suit to match a ring of grey hair. But he's a man with a few surprises – he wears a bushwhacker hat for one, which I see further down the table, and later I discover he is an expert on the ancient and obscure cuneiform b language, the oldest known written language in the world.

On the stand, Andrew Walker describes the expense system he oversees[4] and why the public has no right to see what is going on in his little fiefdom. His elocution is as pinched as the skin on his neck when he looks down to consult his documents, his collar stiffly unforgiving as he shares the following priceless gems with us:

4. At the end of 2009, he was still in position with a salary increase from a band of £115,000–£120,000 to £125,000–£130,000 while Clerk of the House Malcolm Jack saw his salary rise to around £190,000. He also has a grace-and-favour flat, which was upgraded using £100,000 of public money. In a patronage system, there *are* rewards for failure.

'*MPs should be allowed to carry out their duties free from interference . . .*'

'*What you are doing is preparing a peephole into the private lives of a member, which will either distract them or lead them into additional questions which they'll feel they have to defend themselves over.*'

'*Transparency will damage democracy.*'

All this in relation to a speculated reluctance of people wanting to be MPs if they have to account for how they spend public money.

There are plenty of press in the room to witness these statements, and whenever Walker lets loose one of these crackers I watch as the eyes of *The Times*'s political reporter Sam Coates bulge with a mix of shock, outrage and delight. His fingers are flying over his laptop.

In a way I should be grateful for all the Commons' delaying tactics because the timing of my hearing couldn't be better. In the past my battles with the House of Commons had garnered little media interest, but ten days ago the MP Derek Conway was found guilty by the Parliamentary Standards Commissioner of employing his two sons on the public payroll while they were full-time students. Suddenly there is huge media interest in the issue of MPs' expenses. The tide is definitely turning in favour of people's right to know.

Back in court 1, Walker is questioned by the lawyer for the *Sunday Times*, Philip Coppel, before Hugh Tomlinson wades in. This is the first time Andrew Walker has had to answer to the public directly about the operation of the MPs' allowances system and I've planned to make the most of it. The lawyers question Walker forensically about the operation of the Fees Office and what documentation is required for claims and what checks, if any, made to verify their probity. It's here that we begin to uncover the extent to which MPs have been writing their own cheques.

'There is checking where there are receipts. Where there are no receipts there is no checking,' Walker says.

Walker makes a lot about the fact the Fees Office is overseen by the National Audit Office. Hugh asks exactly what constitutes this audit and here we get into the nitty-gritty (which is where the truth lies) and discover that in the last audit only 227 claims were checked, 47 of which were about the additional costs allowances; this is in relation to millions of claims totalling nearly £90 million of public money.[5]

'So that's about three items checked for every £1 million claimed. That does not seem very rigorous,' says Hugh.

'The auditor is not auditing the members,' Walker admits. 'He's auditing us.'

When we press for more details about the additional costs allowance in order to find out precisely what MPs can claim, we discover a 'food rule' that is not written anywhere. We try to prise from Walker the extent of the food allowance. Are receipts required?

'We don't want your Tesco bill if that's what you mean. If it gets more than that [£400] we're beginning to ask: "Is that really necessary?"'

But if the rule is not written anywhere how do MPs know what it is?

Walker remains unfazed. 'My understanding is that

5. Nick Harvey MP, who was at this time on the Members Estimate Committee, described the £87.6 million claimed by MPs as providing taxpayers with 'excellent value for money'.

members are well aware. I am unable to tell you how they are well aware of it.'

Well, at least tell us – is it £400 a week? A month? A quarter? What?

'Unfortunately I don't know.' Walker now begins to look uncomfortable. 'I will have to consult with my colleagues.'

'If you don't know,' Hugh counters, 'I shouldn't think anyone else does.'

I am gleeful – the head of the Fees Office doesn't even know his own rules! It's exactly as I suspected. This is the sort of shoddy rank amateurism that can only exist in secrecy.

Asked if MPs could claim for a large plasma TV (as has been revealed in a *Times* story), Walker says: 'I am glad to say that story was misconceived. It is unlikely we would allow a plasma; we have a price cut-off. A fish tank may be claimable but interestingly a claim was brought to my attention, which I rejected, and iPods we reject – iPods are personal items and not something needed to live away from home.'

Good to see they had some standards.

Hugh then asks Walker: 'But if claims under £250 don't require a receipt how do you know what they are for? Or indeed if they're reasonable?'

Walker: 'If it's below £250 the assumption is that it's going to be reasonable. There are probably rare occasions where we do ask for a receipt.' But he then admits: 'If they claim £100 for food but buy an iPod then we'd still pay them the £100.'

By this point Sam Coates's eyes have practically popped out of his head. He knows he's on to a story here and indeed the next day *The Times*'s front page features a photograph of a fish tank. The *Daily Mail* also run a story.

Walker then lets slip the existence of a 'John Lewis list' which is used in his office as the final arbiter of what is considered a reasonable price for white goods and other furnishings. He is asked to produce a printout of the spreadsheet but tells us: 'It doesn't exist in paper form and whether it can be printed I don't know.' Well, can we see the electronic version? We cannot. Why not?[6]

'The thing is, if it was made public, the maximum price we'll allow for an item, that would become the going rate.'

'So, you're saying that MPs would take advantage?'

Walker doesn't know what to say. But he has to agree or give us the list. He's in a no-win situation.

Hugh continues. 'What you seem to be saying is that you don't trust them. And yet this entire system is based on trust.'

The tribunal members were less than impressed with all this and in ordering full disclosure they described the second homes expense system as 'deeply unsatisfactory', adding that 'laxity of and lack of clarity in the rules for ACA is redolent of a culture very different from that which exists in the commercial sphere or in most other public sector organisations today . . . In our judgement these features, coupled with the very limited nature of the checks, constitute a recipe for confusion, inconsistency and the risk of misuse. Seen in relation to the public interest that public money should be, and be seen to be, properly spent, the ACA system is deeply

6. A reporter from the Press Association quickly wrote a freedom-of-information request for the John Lewis list and gave it to the Commons FOI officer. When this came out in March 2008 it created another media frenzy as the public discover MPs have been claiming for all sorts of appliances and home furnishings.

unsatisfactory, and the shortfall both in transparency and in accountability is acute.'

They ordered the receipts of the fourteen MPs in question to be published. Not only that, we won on the point that the public needed to know the addresses for second homes for which the ACA was being claimed. Ben Leapman made the point that without these addresses, the main abuses of house flipping and mortgage payments would be hidden from the public.

The ruling was so strongly in our favour, I assumed that would be the end of it. We would get our fourteen and then move on to the rest. We'd heard the Commons' own legal team had advised the Speaker there was no point of law to appeal, indeed no point at all. But Michael Martin and the other shady powers lurking in the background were intent on keeping MPs' expenses secret at any cost. They ditched their legal team and hired another – all at taxpayer expense, remember. On the last day allowed for filing an appeal, the House of Commons announced it was going to the High Court.

This was troubling because costs are awarded in this court and they can run into hundreds of thousands of pounds. I rather think such an intimidatory threat of bankruptcy was the primary reason for Parliament launching its appeal. Obviously the Speaker wasn't concerned about costs because he had public money to burn. But I didn't. I wasn't exactly rolling in it. Writers rarely are. I spoke to Hugh and my solicitor Louis Charalambous at Simons Muirhead & Burton. Louis was able to get me legal insurance formulated in such a way that the premium was added onto the back end of the policy so I wouldn't have to pay anything up front. If I lost the case, the insurance would cover my costs. We switched also to a conditional fee agreement, meaning that if I won, the House would have to cover not just my costs but also my insurance and a success fee. Right back at you, Mr Martin. Ben Leapman found a lawyer who would represent him on these same terms.

Our case was expedited and a hearing scheduled for 7 May 2008 before three top judges. It's a unique experience being a party in a High Court case. For such an imposing court the courtrooms are surprisingly cosy. I slid across onto a wooden bench and watched as the barristers came in with their grey-flecked cardboard boxes wrapped with their own branded tape. KBW for the King's Bench Walk lawyers. It's not just one barrister either. At the High Court, one is not enough. You must have two: a senior and a junior barrister, along with the solicitor, of course. I only had one barrister and solicitor but they were more than enough to outgun the four lawyers from the Commons and the Information Commissioner. Hugh Tomlinson spoke for our side in court.

The Commons presented their two favourite arguments: privacy and security. We heard Nigel Giffin QC twist himself in knots trying to argue how it was an unseemly invasion of MPs' privacy for the public to know how MPs spent public money in the course of their public duties. We heard how MPs would likely be shot in their beds if their second-home addresses were made public. No evidence was put forward to indicate any of these threats were anything more than the self-important delusions of a paranoid conspiracy theorist.

'You haven't put forward any evidence as to the reason. That's the difficulty,' the judges had to repeat to the

Commons lawyer on more than one occasion. When the facts don't fit, it's not uncommon for those in authority to suddenly become disaster-movie screenwriters putting forward their delusional imaginings as the only evidence needed.

We argued again that MPs' main- and second-home addresses should be published, putting forward actual evidence of abuses that had occurred when the addresses were kept hidden, such as exposure by the *Mail on Sunday* in 2002 that Michael Trend, a former Conservative MP, had claimed £90,000 for a fictional second home. We argued, too, that every voter has to register on the electoral roll under threat of prosecution so why should MPs be any different? But I wasn't confident the judges would rule in our favour on this point as they are part of the Establishment themselves and haven't been particularly progressive when it comes to the public's right to know.

On 16 May the High Court judges issued their ruling. We'd won! Victory on all counts. Receipts *and* addresses. We had managed to convince not only the Information Tribunal but three High Court judges that MPs, receipts, claims and addresses must be published.

'We are not here dealing with idle gossip, or public curiosity about what in truth are trivialities,' the judges said. 'The expenditure of public money through the payment of MPs' salaries and allowances is a matter of direct and reasonable interest to taxpayers.

'They are obliged to pay their taxes at whatever level and on whatever basis the legislature may decide, in part at least to fund the legislative process. Their interest is reinforced by the absence of a coherent system for the exercise of control over and the lack of a clear understanding of the arrangements which govern the payment of additional costs allowance.'

The receipts were to be published, with only a few specified omissions for genuine private matters (such as health), along with addresses. The judge said that 'there was a legitimate public interest well capable of providing such justification' for the publication.

I walked out of the High Court to a bank of TV and photographic cameras. A few days later, I received the receipts for the fourteen MPs. As suspected there were no privacy or security issues – just embarrassment. Margaret Beckett's bills for gardening, Barbara Follett's for window cleaning, Tony Blair and Gordon Brown getting new kitchens courtesy of the taxpayer. But we had only fourteen MPs. There are 646 in Parliament. What about the rest? I'd asked for them all at the start and if we'd won the right to see receipts for fourteen that should hold true for all. At last it seemed the Commons authorities had got the message and they announced that by October 2008 all receipts for all MPs would be published.

A fantastic victory.

. . . Only they didn't publish and sneakily began to backtrack on their promise.

In July 2008 Conservative MP Julian Lewis put forward a motion, signed by 256 MPs from all parties, exempting from disclosure all MPs' home addresses, their expenditure on security and the identity of anyone delivering goods or services to them. Now bear in mind that all these disaster-movie scenarios had been discussed in both the tribunal and High Court and dismissed for lack of evidence. Where an MP could show actual harm such that he had reported the matter to the police, there is a case for withholding addresses, but in the absence of any facts, the default position should be openness. MPs' addresses are on the electoral roll and on ballot papers so they are hardly secret. That didn't stop Lewis. In the spring of 2009, he tabled an amendment to the Political Parties and Elections Bill so that MPs could keep their addresses secret from the very voters they were supposed to represent, on 'security grounds'. The amendment was carried.

Also in July 2008 a whole raft of expenses reforms promised by Gordon Brown were voted down by MPs. The expenses shake-up would have scrapped the 'John Lewis list' and MPs would have needed receipts for every claim and faced spot checks. Couples would have been blocked from putting in double claims on the same home. All this was scrapped after MPs voted against reform 172 to 144. Oddly enough, for such an important piece of legislation, Brown did not even show up for the vote.

The October 2008 publication date came and went with no receipts forthcoming, nor even a written excuse from Parliament. I phoned up and started asking questions again. The Commons claimed the process was technically 'difficult'. The only thing difficult about it, I thought, was the censoring. That is what required manpower. The less censoring the easier (and cheaper) the job. The Commons said the full set would be published by December 2008, which was also a lie. Here's what was happening behind the scenes.

Around twenty people at a time were working round the clock to black out parts of the expense files. Because MPs were so paranoid about this information getting to the public they specified that only security-clearanced people could do the work. Soldiers and security guards were hired to oversee the scanning and censoring operation, some moonlighting from active duty to earn extra money during their annual leave.

What the managers did not know until months later was that some of the staff were so disgusted by what they saw and by the lies being told to the public about the delays in publication that they made a copy of the data. Between October and December 2008, when the files were sent back for even more censoring, a mole inside the redaction room made a copy and later passed it to John Wick, a former SAS officer. This was just as well because as soon as MPs came back from their lengthy Christmas recess, they began plotting to exempt their expenses from the FOI law again. The idea was to use a statutory instrument so there would be no debate. The change would be retrospective and would have effectively nullified the High Court ruling. Initially the government had cross-party support. I had a call from Ian Drury at the *Daily Mail* who'd learned that Tory leader David Cameron was allowing his backbenchers a free vote on the bill, which was unusual to say the least. It went directly against his public commitment to transparency and expense reform. The *Mail* were thinking of going big on this, he said. I gave my quote and waited. Funnily enough, the next day, Cameron said he didn't support the government's proposal and was urging all his MPs to vote against it. Without Conservative support, the bill was scuppered and the government backed off.

I was at this time making a *Dispatches* programme for Channel 4 called 'The Westminster Gravy Train', broadcast on 19 April 2009. In March, an MP had told me there was a rumour going around Parliament that a disk existed with the expenses data on it. He didn't know any more than that and I had no experience with this sort of illicit method of journalism so I continued to focus my investigation on using the FOI law to prise out whatever information I could get legitimately. (In the States, chequebook journalism is rare. There are only a few papers, such as the *National Enquirer*, that do it and once you've worked for any of them you'll never work on a respectable newspaper again.) We broadcast with several strong stories about MPs using allowances in dubious ways, but we were scrabbling in the dark. Importantly, we didn't have MPs' addresses, nor did we have their receipts. Unbeknown to us, John Wick was just about to hand over a disk with all these details to the *Daily Telegraph*.

On 8 May 2009, a year and a day since my High Court appearance, the *Telegraph* began publishing the full unexpurgated expenses files in daily instalments. The revelations dominated the British media for weeks and you likely know all about that story. The *Telegraph* did a phenomenal job presenting the data, and I don't begrudge them anything even if they did take away my scoop. At least I didn't have to worry about Gordon Brown on the phone every other day and a threatened prosecution. The *Telegraph* were simply doing what a newspaper should do – holding the powerful to account – but what did surprise me was the way the Commons *still* refused to publish the data so everyone could have a look. It was almost as if they were in collusion with the *Telegraph* to keep that paper's circulation up for as long as possible. Only when all the major revelations had been published did the Commons finally let the public see the data but then they did it in such a cack-handed way, blacking out all the scandalous claims, that MPs' expenses became a story all over again. Parliamentarians certainly know how to do bad public relations.

Of course there is more to this story. It's the journalistic equivalent of the golden goose – it gives and keeps on giving. Every few months for the past two years MPs have done something so outrageous or silly they make themselves news yet again. Instead of simply opening up and dealing directly with the citizen they stubbornly clung to their outmoded entitlements and a new quango, the Independent Parliamentary Standards Authority, has been added to an already heaving parliamentary bureaucracy. I see no benefit in this and it's worth pointing out that not one of the misuses of MPs' expenses has ever been exposed through official channels. It has always been via the media through leaks or whistle-blowers.

It is one thing for a politician to say he or she is committed to transparency and direct accountability; it is another entirely to act on those commitments. In the absence of meaningful journalism and direct accountability there is freedom of information. FOI offers a legal approach to get official information out of the hands of those in power. It's important to understand the purpose of FOI, which is, in a nutshell, to prevent and detect corruption. By corruption I mean the misuse of power and public funds by public servants. That must be paramount in our minds. Too many excuses are made to keep information hidden and too often these excuses are accepted as legitimate solely because they come from the mouths of powerful people. Politicians often claim secrecy is necessary for good governance or national security. Very often they have confused their own political interests with what is in the public interest.

Society has an interest in encouraging the efficient use and enforcement of FOI laws and making official information freely available to the public. Uncovering the abuses of the MPs' expense system involved cross-checking thousands of other official records. Instead of this important civic data being freely available, every single search costs money. Land Registry records are essential to confirm land ownership and mortgage details but each address search costs £4 and there is no facility to search by name. It was through land records that the scandal of Elliot Morley's phantom mortgage was uncovered. By checking online electoral rolls and Companies House records, the *Daily Telegraph* team were able to confirm that the Andrew Brown paid thousands of pounds for cleaning services and whose name and address appeared on Gordon Brown's expense receipts was the prime minister's brother.

The net result of all the restrictions and fees on access to public records (as described in Chapter 5) only serves to make such public interest investigation as difficult and costly as possible. This type of journalism is hard graft but provides important information to the public. Yet this is precisely the type of reporting that is near impossible to do in the UK. At least in the case of MPs' expenses, the *Telegraph* had the raw documentation to hand. No media outlet exists in the UK that can spare a reporter the time it takes to get such information through FOI. Everything about the law is stacked against those seeking to get facts legitimately. This is absurd. It simply cannot be made so difficult to expose corruption. The fact is I *did not* actually get the information I originally sought through the law, and that's tragic because it shows that in the UK legal means just do not work. Ironically it is only through illicit means that scandalous corruption can be exposed.

I look at actual sanctions faced by those MPs who abused public funds and see in all cases they are given the benefit of the doubt. At every opportunity their rights to a fair hearing are guaranteed, even overemphasised. What if MPs faced the sort of summary justice Jane Clift faced from Slough Borough Council? Or were under surveillance in the way Mark Kearney and Sally Murrer were from Thames Valley Police? They would rightly protest about such abuses of power, and yet these same people have stood by while private citizens' rights have been trampled.

In the course of these investigations, I came across many people who have done battle with a silent, secretive state, but isn't it surprising that some of the worst silences come from the pinnacle of our supposed democracy? I've told the stories of Francis Irving, Julian Todd and Tom Loosemore, all of whom attempted to drag Parliament into the modern democratic age facing nothing but obstruction for their trouble. This has to change. It is the people who give public servants their power and so it must be the people to whom they are accountable, directly and forthrightly – with no middlemen in between.

Manifesto for a New Democracy

Who am I to put forward a manifesto? I'm not elected. I'm not accountable to any regulator. I'm just a freelance trouble-maker, a rabble-rouser, a nosey parker prying into the silent state, a writer with a love of novels that remind us just how close we are to realising their dystopian fears: Orwell's *Nineteen Eighty-four*, Chuck Palahniuk's *Fight Club*, Margaret Atwood's *The Handmaid's Tale*. Tyler Durden asks in *Fight Club* to be delivered from Swedish furniture; I ask only:

Deliver us from officious officials.

Deliver us from prying bureaucrats who refuse to be named.

Deliver us from arrogant MPs who feel entitled to pilfer the public purse.

In a democracy, everyone has a right to propose ideas and it is in the roiling competition of these ideas that the best become policy and the weakest fall by the wayside. I am not a politician. I can't compel people to give me money to implement my world view. I can't imprison, fine or smear if you don't buy my book or agree with me. I can't siphon off public cash to create a huge PR industry to peddle my propaganda. I have no power other than the facts I've put forward in this book and the belief that if these stories are compelling then they might persuade a few people that our current system isn't acceptable. Things need to change. Here's how:

We should give no more power to the state without the state giving something to us.

Before the state can keep a database of our identities, aggregate our DNA or gather any other intrusive personal information, it should acknowledge that these measures do nothing whatsoever to empower ordinary citizens. We do not need millions of CCTV cameras turning citizens into suspects, nor every child entered into a database.

Name all public officials. These people work for us.

The state should publish its entire staff directory so we can see, *by name,* who is doing what at taxpayer expense.

Throughout this book I've used the real names of real people. If you're going to tell a story then you need to focus on an individual with a name. It's through individuals that we are best able to gain understanding. Yet individuality is precisely what is lacking from the state. A faceless wall of bureaucracy has been built up that alienates citizen from state. If public servants are truly working for the public then we need to know who they are. Wherever we see 'facts' followed by anonymous officials, we should be sceptical. There should be no power exercised without accountability, ending the domination of behind-the-scenes spin doctors and strategists.

This will benefit bureaucracies too. Throughout public services there are professionals with all sorts of expertise, all kinds of information. They have concerns about what works and what doesn't and good ideas for improvement. But in the current anonymised, hierarchical structure these people have no voice. They are not listened to nor trusted and if they dare speak directly to the public they are penalised and often prosecuted. In the end the silent state hurts many for the benefit of an elite few.

Don't believe the hype.

Public relations is about controlling the flow of information in order to sell products. PR has no place in public institutions and drastically damages democracy. Public services are monopolies and without competition they are accountable only through freedom of information and elections. Stop the free flow of information and these institutions stop serving the public. The only ones benefitting from bureaucratic PR are those in power who want to keep it and expand it. These are precisely the people that need to go.

Public information belongs to the people not the state.

Information collected in the name of the public at public expense belongs to the people, not the bureaucracy in which it is housed and not the Monarchy. We need to end the system of proprietary and restrictive copyright of official information. The public shouldn't have to pay multiple times to access necessary civic information held by the Land Registry, Ordnance Survey, Royal Mail, Companies House, Parliament or any other public institution. These institutions have a monopoly on collecting the information, but they should not have a monopoly on its presentation. Free our data.

End privacy profiteering.

We have been sold a lie about privacy protection. We have allowed the state to hide us from each other, stripping us of our identities and alienating us from our neighbours and fellow citizens. We've been sold the idea that we can't be trusted, that only the state can regulate our relationships. All the while the state has greedily accrued knowledge about every single one of us (much of it subjective and overly intrusive) and because the public are locked out from these databases we have no way of knowing what is being collected and no way to stop the relentless profiteering from privacy conducted by the state and those companies it approves.

Open up the courts.

Justice held in secret is no justice at all and yet British courts are in danger of becoming the secret enclave of the rich and powerful. The privatisation of court transcripts, and the numerous restrictions stopping the public seeing justice done, have led to an information class divide between the haves and have-nots. Everyone should have equal access to the courts and court records.

Return to the Peelian Principles.

The police should answer directly to the community – not to politicians and not to Whitehall. The state may have a monopoly on legitimate imprisonment but it should not have the monopoly on policing. Each one of us can do our part to serve as the eyes and ears of the community. The police need to stop seeing citizen action as a threat to their power and instead as a benefit. Robert Peel said it best: the police are the public and the public are the police; the police being only members of the public who are paid to give full-time attention to duties which are incumbent upon every citizen in the interests of community welfare and existence.

Make voting count.

The act of voting has been rendered decorative rather than functional. Democracies should be made up of an informed electorate but currently we have neither information nor a meaningful vote. Voting for our MPs and councillors once every five years isn't enough. Unless we have more information and input into the selection process, we'll continue to see people in power not through merit or because they are good leaders but because they have sucked up to the right powerful people. Deference and patronage still rule the day: politicians and public servants gain and maintain their power not by doing their jobs well or even competently but by staying in favour with those who appointed them. The public should be able to see quickly and easily all the interests bearing down on their elected representatives. If it's public money or affecting public policy then the public have a right to know.

Trust the people.

The issues in this book all grow from a single tragic belief: that the public can't be trusted. The corollary is that the state can. History shows the opposite to be true: individuals on their own do less damage than individuals hidden behind the walls of a faceless institution. The idea that the powerful know best and that we, the general public, can't be trusted with the facts or any real power to manage our own affairs is a pernicious fantasy. It's not irrational to fear the unthinking mob, but the best way to counter this danger is to ensure the electorate are educated and informed. That is why it is so ironic that politicians fight so hard to keep people *un*informed and ignorant.

I put my faith in the kindness of strangers more than the state. I'm no naif: I used to be a crime reporter and I've seen the damage people can do, but in my experience most individuals are good. They become less good when they are stripped of their individuality and told simply to obey orders.

We are not naughty children and the state is not our parent. We should be the masters of public services and as such any dialogue between citizen and state must be on our terms. So shift the balance of power: ask questions, seek facts, challenge authority and don't accept silence for an answer. In a true democracy the state has no right to remain silent.

Acknowledgements

First and foremost: to my agent Karolina Sutton at Curtis Brown and to my wonderfully helpful and insightful editor Drummond Moir at Heinemann. I'm fortunate to have found two fantastic people who saw the vision and were able to make it happen.

As I say in the book, access to information in this country is all about who you know so I'm grateful to know the following: Louis Charalambous, Jeffrey Smele, Lucy Moorman (at Simons Muirhead & Burton); Hugh Tomlinson QC (Matrix Chambers), James Ball and Andrew Bousfield (The Bureau of Investigative Journalism), Nick Davies, Mike Dodd, Matthew Elliott, David Allen Green and Benjamin Pell plus all the other journalists, lawyers and activists who shared their information with me.

Finally thanks to all those who agreed to be interviewed for the book, with particular recognition to those people who found themselves trapped in the teeth of the state and decided to fight back. I couldn't have written this book without you.

Index